I hope ... remind you of ... your great teachers.
Linda Evanchyk,
2003

Those Who Teach
Do More:

Tributes to American Teachers

Merry Christmas to two of the world's best teachers! Thanks for all you have taught our family.
Love,
The Andersons

Written and compiled by
Linda Evanchyk and Carol Mendenhall

ISBN: 1-4033-9398-2 (e-book)
ISBN: 1-4033-9399-0 (Paperback)
ISBN: 1-4033-9400-8 (Dust Jacket)

This book is printed on acid free paper.

1stBooks – rev. 02/21/03

This book has been in the birthing stage for so many years, that there are an equal number of people who deserve our praise and thanks. They are:

Our parents, who were our first teachers.

Our families for listening about this project for years and still agreeing that teachers deserve to be honored every day of the year.

Our friends and colleagues who managed to smile every time we mentioned the latest letter and who have promised to buy "oodles and oodles" of copies of the published book.

Those who responded to our requests and shared their stories.

Elaine Kidwell who made sure the manuscript was as perfect as possible. Will Swords and Randy Pender for creating the cover with an apple that every American teacher would like to receive. Ruth Quigg for the authors' cover photo. Steve Adams for the many hours he dedicated to proofreading to help us get it right.

David Shribman for his foreword.

All the teachers who taught us that the world is waiting for someone who believes in possibilities.

And all the students we have had the pleasure and privilege of teaching and knowing. They are the reason we do what we do.

Table of Contents

Foreword

School's out. And all across the land, windy speakers have been congratulating the graduates. They deserve it. But let's take a moment to congratulate the teachers. They deserve it more.

I have watched (and worshipped) teachers for years. I have two sisters-in-law who are teachers (one math, one physics). I have two daughters who adore their teachers. I have learned very little in life, but I've learned enough to appreciate teachers.

And so today, on the very cliff of summer, it is time-too little, too late-to say thank you.

And to say one thing more: for the past two centuries, American teachers have been mostly idealistic, mostly hard-working, mostly dedicated, and mostly female. That's true today; figures from the National Center for Education Statistics show that 76 percent of public elementary and secondary school teachers are women.

For decades, the greatest beneficiaries of sex discrimination weren't men zooming to the fancy executive suites and the big-salary jobs. No, the greatest beneficiaries of sex discrimination were kids. The women who otherwise might have been brain surgeons or law partners or CEOs became teachers. These women comprised the greatest cadre of teachers the world has ever seen, and if Americans saw far it is because they "stood on the shoulders of giants."

"Teaching attracted extraordinary women," says Diane S. Ravitch, a New York University historian of education. "They believed that the teacher's role was to open students' eyes to great art, great writing, and great deeds. They conveyed a sense of wonder. Their job was a mission."

One great wave of great teachers came during the Great Depression, which as Denis P. Doyle, a Heritage Foundation specialist on education, says, "tipped untold thousands of highly qualified adults into teaching, a group that in more sanguine economic times would have done other things." Those teachers stuck with the profession for the reason that drew them in. There weren't better jobs elsewhere. And here they could make a difference, and did.

Then came the teacher of the postwar boom. The women who took the first tentative steps into the workplace in peacetime – women, of course, had been pressed into factory work during the 1940s – often stepped into schools. They taught Bob Dylan and Bill Clinton, Louise Erdrich and Carly Simon, Jesse Jackson, and Newt Gingrich. They taught future astronauts and computer engineers, poets and protestors, Gulf War heroes and House GOP freshmen.

At the time of the establishment of the Smithsonian Institution, in 1846, John Quincy Adams offered us words that ring true today: "To furnish the means of acquiring knowledge...is the greatest benefit that can be conferred upon mankind. It prolongs life itself and enlarges the sphere of existence."

Some of those people, those enlargers of the sphere of my existence, were, of course, men. There was Mr. DiMento, who taught me where the Kazakh Soviet Socialist Republic was, and his brother, who taught me the quadratic formula. I don't remember a thing about Kazakhstan or the quadratic equation. I remember a lot about the discipline of learning, which I now know was their real lesson. There was Mr. Stromberg, who taught me how a bill became a law, and there was Mr. Kimball, who had the audacity to think the Missouri Compromise and the Spanish-American War were important. I haven't forgotten a thing either man ever said, and I've been enriched by that.

Then there was Professor Slesnick. I never took one of his math courses. No one ever loved me more. There was Coach Lupien. I never played a third of an inning for him. No one ever taught me more. There was Professor Wright. I never missed one of his history lessons. I never made a better investment.

But it is the women I remember best.

Thank you to Miss Waterman, who taught about the life cycle of the butterfly, which I still remember, and about life itself, which I still haven't mastered. Thank you to Professor Gelfant, who taught college students how to read for the first time. Thank you to the Miss White who taught Dickens and to the Miss White who taught trigonometry.

Thank you to Mrs. Rich, who in a terrible November in 1963 tried to explain the inexplicable to unbelieving fourth graders. Thank you to Miss Koury, who introduced me to Aaron Copland.

And thank you to Mrs. Johnson, who this week finished teaching my daughter's second grade in the public schools of the District of Columbia and who every day proved that Henry Adams was right when he said that, "a teacher affects eternity."

Now, more than ever, it is time to revise an old refrain. Let's agree: Those who can, do. Those who teach, do more.

David Shribman
Washington Bureau Chief
The Boston Globe

Shribman was awarded the Pulitzer Prize in journalism in 1995. His own book on great teachers who changed lives is titled, *I Remember My Teacher*, Andrews McNeel Publishing, 2001.

Introduction:

How This Book Happened

Introduction: How this Book Happened

Talk to one hundred teachers and ask them why they teach. You'll hear one hundred different answers, some of which will sound like: it's a calling and only the strong answer the call; it's an art form and the canvas is the student's mind and heart; it's a way to have three months off in the summer; it's a job; it's a way for me to talk about what I love all day and get paid for it; and I want to make a difference in some kid's life the way my favorite teacher made a difference in mine.

Any or all of those reasons could have come from our mouths during the combined fifty-four years we've spent in education—it would depend on the day and how many students had or hadn't turned in homework, paid attention in class, got excited about a novel, laughed out loud at one of our jokes, or forgot the textbook. Being a teacher is the most difficult and the most rewarding job you can have.

Through our careers we have seen the media blame teachers for everything from kids not being able to read to the violence in the streets. On a daily basis, teachers are asked to perform miracles. Charged with preserving the future of the country, we try and open students' minds and hearts to the possibilities of what the future can be. We do that day after day after day. And for what?

Money? Every teacher who is reading this is smiling or laughing now, because money is not what it's about. Prestige? Again, that's a real-knee slapper. No. We do it because we know that somewhere among the multiplication tables, the adverbs, the capitals of the states, and the parts of the cell, we will make a difference in some person's life. And that person will try something for the first time and succeed, will learn to trust an adult, and will want to say thank you to a teacher who helped make one school day, a week, or a year better.

That's why teachers stay in the profession. It's that complicated and that simple. The pages in this book reflect what we've always known about our chosen profession—it's the most important one in the world.

How this book happened is one of those serendipitous stories that happen in life when you're paying attention and watching for possibilities. We met in 1979 when Linda came to Raines High School and started teaching across the hall from Carol. It was Linda's first year—of marriage, of teaching, of being away from home. So, we spent many afternoons in one room or another trying to decide if teaching was the right profession for her. It was, it is, and it always will be. We taught in an inner-city school which created enough challenges and provided enough rewards, that it helped forge our long term-friendship. Even after each of us moved to different parts of the country, our friendship continued. Every time we got together we would reminisce and speculate about writing a book—every teacher has a book of tales. In 1996, the event that would provide the impetus for this book happened.

Our school principal and friend, Jimmie Johnson, retired from Raines. At his retirement reception, which also served as a reunion, several people talked about the difference Mr. Johnson had made in their lives: his colleagues, his former students, and community leaders. At the closing of a very emotional evening, Mr. Johnson spoke. He called his high school English teacher to the podium. This man, who was being honored for his thirty-years as an educator who had been an award-winning coach; who had changed education policy in his district—gave credit for his success to this English teacher who had encouraged him to become an educator. Mr. Johnson realized, as we all do, that it all goes back to that one person who makes a difference and changes our destiny. And on this, his retirement night, he publicly acknowledged this teacher.

That one moment had such impact on us, that we began discussing the influence teachers had had on us. We remembered teachers from elementary school, junior high, high school, and college who had given us encouragement, and who had opened up possibilities for us. We moved from that discussion to one about successful people and how all of them must have had a teacher who influenced them.

We were inspired to share Mr. Johnson's story and when we did other teachers and friends began to share their "teacher who made a difference" story. Although the stories were different, teachers were the heroes in the tales. We learned that teachers can be heroes by giving a smile, by explaining something so clearly it finally clicks, by believing in potential, and by giving fifty cents for lunch money.

All of the stories inspired us and we began to write down people's stories and to send letters to celebrities and other individuals who enjoy success. The first response we received was from Florida State University football coach Bobby Bowden. His story about his third grade teacher, Irene Pierson, who taught him to sign his name, verified what we knew--that everyone, even the rich and famous, has been positively influenced by a teacher.

Coach Bowden is successful enough in his chosen career that people pay him to sign his name. In his story he tells why he signs his name as legibly as he can. Not just because Miss Pierson taught him the mechanics of handwriting but because she taught him the importance of pride in a name and signature. Miss Pierson instilled a value that Coach Bowden has carried with him through his life.

As we continued to query well-known individuals we were amazed at the heart-warming stories we received. People in varying careers and positions recalled teacher after teacher who showed love for them, imparted wisdom to them, stood as a model of values for them, or opened the world of possibilities to them.

The Supreme Court Justice, the professional coach and athlete, the entertainer, the top-selling writer, the government official and others all had that teacher who had made a difference. This book is a way of thanking those teachers and all the teachers who have gone beyond the hall passes and the homework to become hometown heroes to thousands.

Every time we open a letter and read these stories, we feel the power teachers possess. Those of us in education all hope we are having such a positive impact on our students today.

To the student considering a career in education, let this book be one of encouragement. To the teacher who wonders if he or she is truly making a difference, let this book be one of affirmation that you are. To anyone who questions whether the American Education System is still working, let this book be one of reassurance. To those who have forgotten the joys of being a student, let this book be one that brings back great memories. And to everyone who hasn't done so, let this book be a reminder to thank that special teacher.

Linda Evanchyk and Carol Mendenhall

Section One:
Our Experiences as
American Teachers

The Decision to Teach

Carol's Story:

Teaching wasn't my first choice as a profession. When I was seven I decided to be a nun and wore a towel wrapped around my head for at least a week. I went around making signs of the cross and using the salad dressing as holy water. My mother had finally had enough and explained to me that you had to be a Catholic to be a num and we weren't. So, that ended my first foray into choosing a career. I forgot all about it until I heard a speech by a motivational speaker explaining that if you didn't know what you life would be, you would wind up a failure. Can you believe someone would say that to young people!

That one remark had such impact on me, I decided right there I would be an English teacher. I was in the seventh grade and English was my favorite subject. So, driven by fear of failure or just plain fear, my life's work was chosen. Once I'd made up my mind, I never changed. I'm amazed at that now since I seem to take forever deciding what to eat for lunch. Being decisive is a blessing bestowed on the young and uninformed, I've concluded.

Linda's Story:

Becoming a teacher is what happened to me on my way to pursuing a journalism degree. True, as a child, I played "school" just as many children do. I was always the teacher. I enjoyed being in charge. I have always liked the school environment, and if I could make a living doing so, I would change from being a teacher to being a student.

During summers I received copies of the *Weekly Reader* in the mail. I loved these little newsy magazines. I always thought I would like to write an article for the magazine. Even at a young

2

age I knew that it must be a thrill to have something I had written in print. That's probably when the journalism bug bit me.

In junior and senior high school I was able to see my writing in print through student publications. I also got to teach (in a sense). As an editor on the school newspaper and yearbook, I trained other staff members.

My sophomore year in college I took an Introduction to Education class mainly because a professor I had for a creative writing class suggested I take the course as one of my elective credits. I admired this teacher and thought the class might be fun, so I registered for it. The first day of class the teacher had each student tell why he or she wanted to be a teacher. When my turn came, in my 19-year-old cockiness I indicated, "I don't want to be a teacher. I plan to be the next Barbara Walters." I cringe at my arrogance and the implication I made that the journalism profession was superior to the teaching profession. Luckily, the teacher saw my statement as one of confidence and motivation and he nurtured both my writing skills and my enthusiasm.

As the semester went along I enjoyed the experiences I was getting through the class. I spent many hours in various classroom settings, and I found being with students of all ages a thrill. By the end of the semester I knew I wanted to teach, and I decided then that I wanted to share my love of writing with students, and hopefully open doors for them so they could know the thrill of seeing their writing in print.

Getting Into the Classroom

Carol's Story:

Education classes cannot possibly prepare you for what happens in the classroom when you're the one responsible for the learning of other people, but they're what we use as the practice step. For every one of my education classes, I had to do a practicum. So I was an aide in the third grade classroom during the "open school" concept—no walls. Eight year olds were supposed to ignore 100 other third graders and pay attention to the subtleties of multiplying and dividing. Another of my experiences was in a middle school in the inner city of Denver. On my first day there, I was standing in the hallway when a young man came up to me and asked me if I was a lost Girl Scout, and then he laughed with all his friends. I didn't get it until I looked at what I was wearing—Girl Scout green, including knee socks (it was a long time ago, and the knee socks were in style).

My fondest memory of that experience was a young man I tutored in reading. We didn't do a lot of reading when we met once a week, but we did do a lot of talking—about his family, football, and his career in the NFL. After three weeks, his teachers started telling me how much better he was doing and that I should just keep doing whatever I was doing. That was a great lesson for me—caring and developing relationships are two of the most important aspects of teaching.

By the time I actually did my student teaching, I felt like an old hand at this teaching thing. Then I had my first day **alone** with the kids—eleventh grade students studying science fiction. I thought I had planned this great lesson and couldn't wait to start it. But they didn't want to do it and they just ignored me. Oh, they were watching me and even occasionally answering a question, but they were also deciding what they were going to do after school, that weekend, and in the next class. I can still remember that feeling—helplessness. It was in that moment, I learned another great lesson in teaching—you never have control—it's an illusion—but one you've got to cultivate if you're going to survive. I don't know how I did it, but I learned how to capture attention at the beginning of the class and keep it rolling and I also learned to laugh—and I did that more everyday.

Linda's story:

Student teaching is a rite of passage. It is where theory meets reality. I had taken all the courses and written model lesson plans. It was time for the last challenge before receiving a college degree and a teaching certificate.

The teacher who was my student teaching mentor had been teaching for several years and had a challenging teaching schedule: British Literature, Introductory Drama, Advanced Drama, and a competitive Speech class. It was exactly what I had hoped for because I didn't want to spend the day teaching the same lesson repeatedly, and because I did not see myself as a strong lecturer, but more of an activities teacher.

My student teaching experience was far from a "stand and deliver" one. That semester the British Literature classes acted out Shakespearean scenes; the drama classes put on two different plays—a children's fairytale, and a crime spoof; and the members of the speech class traveled to several forensic tournaments—on school buses. It was probably the best experience I could have had to prepare me for my teaching career. I learned how to work on several projects simultaneously and how to get organized so that each project was a success.

Through these activities I experienced the feeling of being part of a student's success. I remember vividly the opening night of one of the plays. A huge case of stage fright gripped one of the students who had a leading part. I stood in the stage wings with this student who had a death grip on one of my arms, and who told me she could not go on because she felt that she would open her mouth and she would throw up. I consoled her and told her she could handle it and when it came time for her entrance, I got her to let go of my arm and I gently pushed her onstage. Not only did she not get sick, but she performed her part superbly.

The entire semester I had the privilege of being a part of the students' success. It made all those extra hours of practice, working on sets, preparing lesson plans, and traveling on school buses to forensics meets all worthwhile when the students performed their best.

I knew at the end of that semester that I had made the perfect choice of a career, and I was eager to get a teaching position and to start succeeding with my "own" students.

That First Year Teaching

Carol's Story:

Statistics about teaching reveal that 50% of teachers leave the profession in the first three years. Startling—unless you've ever been the one standing in front of 30 seniors on the first day of school wondering what possessed you to think you could enlighten this group to the wonder of great literature.

I can still remember my greatest fear—that no one would listen to me and they would just leave after about 10 minutes. So, keeping them in the class became my goal. I had eight pages of first day instructions to get through—from getting an accurate roll (which was harder than you think), to making sure the free and reduced lunch forms were passed out without prejudice (whatever that means).

Luckily, the students had been through this more recently than I had and they helped me with it—I came through my first day unscathed.

The first time I had to discipline a student, I shook-again the fear that I wouldn't be taken seriously. It was such a relief when Cassandra came in after school and did what I told her.

I was blessed with a great mentor who told me that when you see a spark in a student's writing fan it and you will be amazed at what will happen. My first year I had students who were some of the best writers I've ever taught. Their poetry humbled me in its simplicity and depth. Their natural rhythm patterns in the language made reading assignments a joy—I actually looked forward to grading papers. I'm smiling while I'm writing this because I can still feel that thrill of reading a student's words and being 'blown away' by them.

I wasn't a particularly good teacher that first year as far as teaching techniques are concerned. I really just tried to get through each day without incident. But I was a great teacher when it came to belief in my students and the importance of my subject and because of that I still hear from that first group. They allowed me to learn with and from them and never made me feel like a rookie and I owe them thanks for that.

Linda's Story:

My first year of teaching was also a "first" year for other areas of my life. I had been married only two months when school opened that year, and it was the first time I had lived in a large city away from family and friends. I was running on enthusiasm and found I had to get tough fast.

The first two individuals I met are the two who also had the most influence on my initial success as a teacher. Jimmie Johnson is the former principal who hired me that first year. In our initial hour-long interview he evidently saw something in this naïve, idealistic, small-town young woman that he felt would lead to success for me and for students. I'm sure I answered "yes" to some of his questions when I had no idea exactly what he was asking me to do! I was so ready to get started I probably would have agreed to take on almost any task to get the job.

The first day of school for teachers that year I met Carol Mendenhall, who was the chairperson of the Language Arts Department. From that day she took me under her wing and helped me refine my teaching style and skills. Just as Jimmie Johnson had done, Carol saw possibilities in me that I could not recognize and she became my friend and mentor.

My first year's teaching schedule was one of real contrast. I had several classes of tenth grade students who had very weak reading and writing skills. Indeed, many were functionally illiterate. I also had a journalism class where students produced the school newspaper. I was excited to be working with journalism again, and with intelligent, motivated students who could write. That staff was part of my salvation when, many days, I felt incompetent due to seeing little or no progress with the students in my English classes, and when I questioned my ability to teach.

Several times Carol gave me pep talks when I'd sit in her classroom after school pleading, teary-eyed, for her to tell me how to reach the low-level students. More than anything she convinced me that I was on the right track, to be patient and to approach the students in the English classes as I did my student journalists. Carol's words finally began to make sense to me. I realized I was a different person in my journalism class. I was myself—with a sense of humor and a real personality. So, with a little fear, I took off my "teacher" face and let the students meet the real me. And...they liked me, and I discovered I liked them. I had let my desire for the students' success take over the enjoyment of learning for all of us.

Despite the fact that I had convinced myself that I would surely be fired if all the students didn't end the year as proficient writers, I stuck with Carol's advice and slowly success came. While none of the students had any of their writing published that year, a majority passed the standardized competency test in English—thereby getting credit for the course. More importantly, true progress could be seen in their reading and writing skills.

In addition, I entered the school newspaper into competition sponsored by the city's newspaper. Previously the journalism program from our school had not received much recognition. Our staff received second place in the high school division, and when the student editor got up to accept the award it was as if we had all won a Pulitzer.

I worked very hard that year, and I indeed did grow up. I probably learned more than my students did that year. Not only did I begin to learn how to teach, but I learned mostly about myself. I knew I had the desire to teach, and at the end of that first year I knew that I truly was a teacher, and had made a difference in students' lives.

It's amazing how now, more than twenty years later, I can remember so many of those "first year" students so vividly.

Our Teachers

Carol's Story

Teachers are in the business of helping students realize their dreams; one of the major ingredients to that is caring enough about them to care what their dreams are. When I was teaching at Madison High School I learned about the power of caring and compassion from Mr. "D," the man who taught next to me. He told me this story:

He was teaching a class of 11th grade gifted English students. He had spent weeks preparing for this class, re-reading the novels, creating what he considered challenging essays, lectures, and other experiences for the students. But the class wasn't responding the way he thought they should. Some of them were, in fact, completely disinterested. They didn't participate in the discussions, their essays were sloppy, and they "yawned" in his face. Finally, he'd had it and he decided to ask the class what the problem was and what could he do to make it a better experience for them. After a passionate plea about scholarship and knowledge, he ended with "what do you want from me?" The room resounded with silence. Finally, a brave young lady dared to raise her hand. He called on her. Her answer, "Just *like* us, Mr. D. Just *like* us." He couldn't believe it was that simple, but it was.

And for that class, it was the beginning of real scholarship once they "were liked."

Linda's Story

Helen Nash was the definitive English teacher. She was demanding, but not unrelenting. As a sophomore in her honors-level English class, I was challenged daily to attain the standards she set forth. Mrs. Nash was a few years older than several of my other high school teachers, and her maturity was a good match for my immaturity.

She impressed me as one of the most intelligent teachers I had ever had and her knowledge of the English language, as well as the life experiences she shared, helped me mature as a young teenager and writer.

It was obvious to all of us in her class that she loved teaching and loved us. Mrs. Nash has a terrific Southern drawl that was mesmerizing. If you closed your eyes, you were on the set of Gone With the Wind. She called all her students "Honey," as if everyone had the same first name. She smiled even when she was reprimanding us, as if she saw hope in us even with our sophomoric flaws.

When Mrs. Nash put the final approval on one of my essays, I knew that I had done a great job. The ultimate approval came from Mrs. Nash several years later, however. There was an article in the local newspaper about a pen pal program another teacher and I developed to use to promote literacy skills. I received a copy of the newspaper article along with a letter from Mrs. Nash, part of which read, "I am very, very proud of you! As soon as I saw the article I said, 'She's one of mine!' To see one of my former students perform so well is an intrinsic reward that is precious to me."

I still have that letter and others she has sent over several years. Mrs. Nash had already retired when I came back to my high school to teach, but we still correspond on a regular basis.

Of the accolades I have been fortunate to receive from my teaching endeavors, none means more than the handwritten notes of love and encouragement I have received from Mrs. Helen Nash.

When her name is mentioned from time to time, I am proud to borrow her line and say, "She's one of mine!"

Section Two: Tributes to American Teachers

To preserve the integrity of the stories sent to us by the individuals in this book, only minor editing was done. The stories within were written from the heart of each contributor.

Valerie Ackerman
President, Women's National Basketball Association

I'll never forget my high school Latin teacher, Kate Thursby. She was quintessentially British, with an air that set her apart from all the other teachers at my suburban New Jersey school. Mrs. Thursby was no-nonsense in the classroom: she demanded effort, and her eyes would cloud over if it became apparent during our daily drills that one of us hadn't done the previous night's homework assignment.

But although she was strict in her way, no teacher I ever had was more passionate about her subject, and none could match Mrs. Thursby's ability to entertain, as she regularly regaled us with stories about the great historical figures of the Roman Empire. And although she was largely formal in her dealings with people, her affection for her students was apparent in the way she always referred to us as "deah" whenever she called on you. I went on to take Latin in college, but without Kate Thursby to infuse the course with life, I couldn't sustain the interest. Mrs. Thursby made such an impression on me that even today I remember much of what she taught me (*veni, vidi, vici*). She was simply a gem, and my education wouldn't have been the same without her.

Kim Alexis
Model

I actually remember a lot of my teachers. My mother kept in touch with my first grade teacher Mrs. McCormick for years. She saw me prosper in New York and followed my career.

Also my swim coach from the YMCA through the years has kept in touch. Bill Natmeier even came to my awards ceremony in my hometown of Lockport, NY when I got an Historic Walk of Fame brick (He took a lot of pictures).

Mr. Copelass was also a great inspiration. He was my English teacher and he pushed me to be my best always. He later confided to my mom that he worried that he might have pushed too far but I rose to his challenge.

Robert E. Allen
Chairman of the Board, AT&T

I graduated from New Castle Chrysler High School in 1953 and, although it's a tough choice, my two favorite teachers would be Mrs. McCord, my English teacher, and Juanita Rucker, my speech teacher. In today's high-tech business world, I've found that written and verbal English skills are more important than ever. Good communications skills are a competitive asset to corporations and a career asset to individuals.

Each of these teachers made great demands on me and taught me to make great demands on myself.

Steve Allen
Comedian/Entertainer

That the American educational process is considerably less than perfect is acknowledged by everyone. But those who conclude that because of its inadequacies it makes sense to simply walk away from it are doing two very destructive things. First of all they are harming themselves, placing themselves under dreadful handicaps from which they could never possibly recover during the rest of their lives, and secondly they are doing harm to the fabric of American society since if there's anything we do not now need it is an even larger number of citizens who are strikingly ignorant.

In my own youth I was fortunate enough to attract the attention of two particular teachers who, by nothing more than taking a personal interest in me, did me a great deal of good.

One was a Catholic nun, Sister Mary Seraphia, who discovered, when I was in 7th grade and 8th grade, that I had the ability to write. Sister Seraphia made me the editor of a little school paper and encouraged my writing in other ways. Because I was born with a fairly high IQ, I had never had much difficulty in at least passing tests and getting good marks. But this kindly teacher's personal interest in me was extremely helpful.

Much the same thing happened a few years later when I was attending Hyde Park High School in Chicago. An English teacher, Marguerite Byrne, discovered that I was missing classes and not taking advantage of some of those I was attending. She encouraged me to write, to submit my poetry to the *Chicago Tribune*, to enter an essay contest, made me the editor of a school magazine, and in other simple ways helped to guide me in the right direction.

Even after having had the benefit of her wise counsel I still occasionally missed classes but did not spend the time in neighborhood pool halls, theaters, or beaches. Instead I went to the nearby Museum of Science and Industry or to either the school or neighborhood libraries, where I read everything I could get my hands on.

From that date to this I have been passionately concerned about the large process of education, not only for myself, but for the American people. A number of my books—for example one called *Dumbth: And 81 Ways to Make Americans Smarter*—have provided a means to express my views on this issue.

William L. Allen
Editor, National Geographic

I was fortunate to have such a wealth of dedicated, caring teachers from kindergarten through high school that I remember virtually every one.

There were Miss Little and Miss Drake in the 3rd and 4th grades who skirted rules to give me extra work from higher grades.

The two Miss Marshes—Miss Mittie and Miss Sarah—were legends. Miss Mittie called us all Mr. and Miss. Miss Sarah gave us punctuation and grammar rules that I can still recite from memory, i.e. "The modifier of a gerund is in the possessive case."

Miss Kirkham, first among equals, guided us in the 7th grade, and can still remember the name and reading group of every one of us in her class 43 years later.

When my mother passed away in 1995, I stood in the sand and grass burrs of a small East Texas country cemetery greeting old friends. As I looked up, supported on the arm of her younger brother was Miss Kirkham, still stern, elegant and caring, holding her 90-something body as straight as we all remembered. "Your mother supported everything we ever wanted for the schools. She was a special person to us all. We loved her." She had asked to be driven sixty miles to tell me that. That is special.

Wally Amos
Founder, Famous Amos Cookies

I remember a special teacher I had in Junior High School named Miss Webster. She was fun, she made us all feel special and that we could learn. She made a big difference in my life and I am thankful for her.

Lynn Anderson
Country Music Singer

Occasionally, I wonder where Marjorie McLain is...what she's doing, how's her health 'n stuff. Mrs. McLain was my teacher forever, it seems. Well, at least through four years of high school and a year of college. And I totally believe it goes further.

Mrs. McLain was my English teacher at Bella Vista High, CA. She taught the accelerated programs and served as advisor for both the school newspaper and the yearbook. I saw her a LOT. Made Editor as a Junior, remained such as a Senior and (be darned if she didn't move to the same college I chose) as a Freshman. Not that it was all roses. She and my chemistry teacher busted my prideful straight A butt a week before graduation for using a news pass signed "McL." to cut school for lunch with Jim. Blew my editor gig, dumped me from Student Council, cost me my Valedictorian speech at graduation. Never forgot, did I?

I never made it in the journalism business. Somehow that record contract distracted me. But guess what? My daughter majored in English and Journalism...went to Oxford; worked as a UPI stringer out of London; now runs her own P.R. firm in Nashville.

Was it me...or was it Marjorie?

Paul Anka
Singer, Songwriter

I was schooled primarily in Canada. I will always be grateful to one of my first teachers. I must have been in first or second grade at the time. Though I don't remember her name, she encouraged me to pursue my creative side. I will always be indebted to her because it was her initial support that helped me to develop my writing skills."

Piers Anthony
Science Fiction Author

I was once a high school English teacher myself, so I have a notion of your trade.

How much of my success was owed to a key teacher I'm not sure. I've always been fairly independent, and pretty much forged my own path. But I did appreciate the help of one of my teachers in college. He was Will Hamlin, and for a time I had a course in creative writing with one teacher, him, and just one student: me. With that kind of instruction, I learned a good deal, and later did achieve my dream of writing professionally. I also appreciated Will Hamlin's courage when there was stress between the student body and the college faculty that got me suspended and came close to shutting down the college. Will was the only faculty member who had the moral stamina to stand up for the rights of the case rather than hewing to the official faculty position, perhaps putting his tenure at risk. Decades later, when I became a major financial supporter of the college, I reminded them of that. Will was there when I needed him, in more than one sense.

Lance Armstrong
Professional Cyclist, Four-Time Tour de France Winner

Well, I wish I would have paid better attention in Spanish class, but really my biggest inspiration when I was young was my swim coach named Chris MacCurdy. He was tough and organized, I hated it at the time – he was a very focused and driven person (1986 – I was around 15). I thought he was crazy! If I only knew then what I know now... in hindsight he's the best coach I've ever had. The great thing is that we've kept in close contact, and now he's one of my best friends.

Lucie Arnaz
Actress

All it takes is one nasty, mean, unthinking punitive teacher to kill a child's thirst for learning. Or <u>one</u> supportive, imaginative, fiercely strict and unconditionally loving teacher to instill a joy of learning and a secure sense of self that will carry them through a life time.

Courteney Cox Arquette
Actress

I am delighted to write to you about a teacher who made a difference in my life. Her name is Sandy Newton and she taught Distributive Education when I was in the 11th grade at Mountain Brook High School in Birmingham, Alabama.

There isn't just one story about Ms. Newton that I could tell, but, rather, many because, truth be told she was more than just a teacher. She was a special friend and confidante who was more like a member of the family. She was "one of the gang," as my mom says, and I remember her energy and fun-loving spirit with a smile on my face. She was a special person who made me feel like a special person, and that has to be one of the greatest gifts that any teacher can give a student.

Edward Asner
Actor

After graduating from Mark Twain grade school, I entered Wyandotte High to join 2,000 other kids. I felt very intimidated and felt at sea at losing our tight little group at Mark Twain.

19

Somehow I blundered through freshman year but my study habits were rotten and my grades very average. I'd become a clown.

By sophomore year it was getting worse! Until the full power of Miss Louise Timmer began to take effect. She was a character out of Dickens. In winter, her cheeks would turn a bright red along with her nose, which would produce a steady drip that she would dab at in the nick of time. She ran a tight ship and when someone would act up or misbehave, she'd have them learn and recite a poem of her choosing in front of the class. Guess who ended up doing the most reciting?

Out of this labor I began to get a grip on myself and knew I had to start buckling down in all departments. I acquired study habits; I was determined to become an achiever and out of Miss Timmer's punishment I found I had a knack for memorization, and my skill in reciting long poems awed my classmates. From this distant beginning I think I traveled down a long trail until I finally, happily found myself an actor, reciting <u>many</u> long poems.

Miss Timmer, you were a doll and I'll always be grateful for your effect on my life.

Chet Atkins, C.G.P.
Guitarist

After many years I still have fond memories of Mabel Berry who introduced me to the writings of Mark Twain, an author I continue to collect and read.

Pete Babcock
Vice President/General Manager, Atlanta Hawks
Basketball Team

My 7th grade and 8th grade teachers, Mrs. Dowd and Mr. Hume (Holiday Park Elementary School, Phoenix, Arizona,) were both inspirational individuals whose love of teaching came through to all their students.

My sixth grade teacher, Ralph Morrison of Katherine Lee Bates Elem. School in Colorado Springs, CO, was probably my most memorable. He had a way of making learning truly fun and constantly challenged us to improve. I was able to keep in touch with him for a number of years and did visit him when I first got into the NBA.

In high school, I was strongly influenced by several coaches. Royce Yower and Jerry Waugh, basketball coaches at Maryvale High School in Phoenix.   Both taught us the importance of maximizing your potential as an individual and how to effectively contribute to the greater good of the team.

I was fortunate to have many good teachers along the way; and they all played a major role in my development.

Joan Baez
Singer, Songwriter, Activist

When Joan went back to her grammar school about 8 years after she had graduated, she was doing a singing tour in her own home town, one of her teachers button-holed me and showed me a picture Joan had drawn to illustrate what she had learned about Charles Dickens. This was an exam they were to be graded on and the teacher said the faculty couldn't decide whether to expel her from English class or what to do with her. She said, "It was that way all the time with her. She never had her homework, but when it came time to answer questions relative to the lesson,

Joan always came up with a picture that showed that she knew exactly what was going on in the book." So they never put her out. They kept her pictures and that particular teacher made copies of her English exam that night of the concert and put one on every seat. What does a mother do when her daughter never opens a textbook, but still seems to understand what the teacher is talking about?

I'm afraid I did nothing. No use, she could out-argue me any old time and I don't think her father was aware of her antics at school. I hope not. She did graduate!

(Joan was on concert in Europe, so Joan Baez's mother graciously submitted this story.)

Dave Barry
Columnist, *The Miami Herald*

I wrote a lot in high school – mostly essays in English class, but also a couple of humor columns for the school paper. One teacher in particular – I remember her only as Mrs. Adams, because of course in high school you can't comprehend the idea that teachers have first names – liked my writing and strongly encouraged me to do more. I fondly remember Mrs. Adams, who encouraged me to try to be funny in my writing and would sometimes read my essays to the class. I was too embarrassed to read them myself. In fact, I'm still too embarrassed to read them myself, so I just put them in the newspaper. I hope Mrs. Adams is still reading them. This is, in part, why I became an English major in college, and ultimately a newspaper columnist.

Lawrence K. Beaupre
Editor, *Cincinnati Enquirer*

In September of my senior year, in 1965, I was playing sandlot football and was tackled hard. I severely broke my collarbone and was hospitalized for four days after surgery. My senior English teacher, Sister Mary Louise, visited me in the hospital. She brought me a book of Chekhov short stories and we talked. She asked me about my plans upon graduation. I told her my vague ideas. She wondered why I didn't want to go to college. Well, I hadn't really thought about it, I told her. She said she thought I had talent as a writer and should be considering something like journalism. After I was released, I decided – still rather tenuously – that I would apply to a journalism school. For money reasons, I narrowed my sights to the University of Illinois. It turned out that it had a fine journalism school, I became editor-in-chief of the college newspaper, stayed on for a master's degree and was in some demand for a job. I will never forget the favor she did me, and I am deeply grateful. I have no idea where I would be in life today without her kind interest in me. To this day, I am deeply respectful of teachers and their ability to influence young people at critical points in their lives.

As for Chekhov: I confess that I never did read the book.

As for Sister Mary Louise, I owe her my career.

Yogi Berra
Member, Baseball Hall of Fame

I had a wonderful teacher, her name was Miss West. She came to watch me play ball, and supposedly always knew I would be in the Major Leagues. She let me sneak my mitt into class, and helped me with my homework. All the kids loved her.

Bonnie Blair
Olympic Speed Skater

I recall a game called "Smarty Pants" that my 6th grade teacher had her students play. This game was similar to Trivial Pursuit. It was fun for the kids and a great way to learn. Even now I find myself remembering things that we learned playing "Smarty Pants."

Kenneth H. Blanchard
Author, Speaker, *One Minute Manager*

I see emotional attachment as a problem not only in business, but in schools with teachers, and at home with parents. They often want to be liked. As a result, they may back off from decisions that would push people to be their best. Few of us enjoy making the kind of intervention in which people might get mad at us. And yet, when you think back, the people who were most influential in your life were probably the ones who got into your face when you needed it.

I remember an English teacher named Miss Symmes. All the other English teachers I had had would pat me on the back and give me a B because they liked me and wanted me to like them. Not Miss Symmes. The first essay I wrote for her she returned with an F and told me I was better than that. Since I was already a student leader, I thought I could get by with my gift for gab, but she insisted that I needed to learn to write, too. And she wouldn't back off. She pushed me and pushed me until, on the last paper I turned in to her, she was proud to give me an A. I was proud too. I'll never forget her. I bet you have a "Miss Symmes" in your life.

Judy Blume
Author

When I was a junior at Battin High School in Elizabeth, New Jersey, Albert Komishane made English the class I most looked forward to each day. He wasn't afraid to laugh with us, to relax with us, to hear what we had to say. In his class we were encouraged to think, to explore, to be creative. When we studied a unit on the history of ballads, we wrote our own and performed them in front of the class. I wrote not one, but three ballads, because Mr. Komishane's enthusiasm for the subject was contagious. I loved writing those ballads! I can still sing them... but only in the shower.

I can't say whether being in his class influenced me or if it affected my personal or profession life. But I can say that I enjoyed every moment in his class, that I think of him fondly and I have always been happiest when involved in creative projects. Mr. Komishane encouraged my efforts, provided a nurturing class atmosphere and enjoyed us as much as we enjoyed him. At least he made us feel that way. What more can a student ask for in a teacher? I only wish I'd had more like him. Thank you, Mr. Komishane!

By the way, he showed up at our 40th high school reunion looking as if he'd hardly aged. And he still had that great laugh.

Robert Bly
Writer, Poet

GRATITUDE TO OLD TEACHERS
When we stride or stroll across the frozen lake,
We place our feet where they have never been.
We walk upon the unwalked. But we are uneasy.
Who is down there but our old teachers?

Water that once could take no human weight—
We were students then—holds up our feet,
And goes on ahead of us for a mile.
Beneath us the teachers, and around us the stillness.

Pat Boone
Singer, Actor

Mack Craig was a singular influence on my life—greater than any other human influence, with the exception of my parents.

Mack was the young principal of David Lipscomb High School, a Christian "oasis" in Nashville, Tennessee where I grew up. Most of my grammar school friends went to secular high schools, but I worked for my Dad in the construction business in the summertime to pay my own way through a Christian high school. My thinking then was that I <u>needed</u>, as a young man, daily Christian instruction in the Bible and living, as well as "head knowledge." That's why David Lipscomb existed—and still does.

Mack was one of those wonderful human beings who saw every student as a precious and valuable and unique life, waiting to be shaped into something magnificent. He taught Latin, which I took 4 years, and was well versed in all subjects. A gifted administrator, he also had a great sense of humor and led the singing and took part in all the fun activities during our school year. All the kids saw him as a friend and counselor, not just their principal.

We grew especially close, because he saw in me a deep desire to make my life count for God in this world, and wanted to nourish that. Through his oversight and encouragement, I was cartoonist and sports editor for our high school paper, and ran for and won the Presidency of each of my classes, and finally the Student Body itself, and also landed a weekly radio show on a top station in Nashville! Mack went to the owner of the station and proposed the idea of a teen talent show, with this young Pat Boone as singer/host. And WSIX bought the idea!

Mack, in our many private counseling sessions and discussions, always addressed every vital decision I had to make with, "Is it right?" All other considerations aside, all wishes and hopes and pressures pushed to the background, "Is it right?"

That piercing and wise question helped me make a lot of good decisions in high school, and ever since. Because of Mack, I had decided I wanted to be a teacher/preacher like he was, but God had a different idea for me. My singing hobby took over while I was in college, and a career exploded, so that when I graduated from Columbia University in 1958, I already had million dollar/movie/TV recording contracts. I also had four daughters! Mack married Shirley and me, and it "took."

Mack will always loom in my life as my principal role model, after my own Mom and Dad. I devoutly wish every young person could have a teacher and friend like Mack Craig.

Bobby Bowden
Head Football Coach, Florida State University

Every time I sign my name I think of Irene Pierson. She was my writing teacher in the third grade at Barrett Grammar School in Birmingham, Alabama. Actually, every time I sign my name I think of Miss Pierson and my older sister Marion. Both are deceased now but I am reminded of them both daily. It was in 1939 that Miss Pierson taught me to sign my name legibly. She would spend day after day in writing class giving drills and showing us the rhythm in writing.

Where my sister comes in is Miss Pierson taught her to write several years before me and Marion had absolutely the prettiest handwriting I have ever seen. I always wished I could write like her. Last week I sat down and signed my name 1,000 times and it took me about three hours. With each signature I unconsciously asked myself is this the way Miss Pierson would want it? Is this the way my sister would do it? Is this as clear and distinct as Marion would do it? Don't get me wrong, I'm not signing my name 1,000 times for practice but because I get paid for it.

Some people scribble their name when they sign autographs and you can't read it at all. My dad taught me the most valuable asset I had was my <u>NAME</u>. When I sign signatures I sign it as legible as I can, like Marion and like Miss Pierson would have wanted me to do 60 years ago.

Ed Bradley
Journalist – *60 Minutes*

I have had many wonderful teachers over the years. I just did an interview for a newspaper story about a college professor who is now in his nineties. At a difficult period in my life he was instrumental in my college education. However, in response to your request, I would go back to my early years. Sister Ignacita was at the same time a harsh disciplinarian, enthusiastic supporter and a wonderful educator. She said to me in the fourth grade, "You can be anything you want to be." And I believed her.

Pat Brady
Cartoonist

ROSE IS ROSE © by Pat Brady
ROSE IS ROSE reprinted by permission of United Features
Syndicate, Inc.

Terry E. Branstad
Former Governor, Iowa

My eighth grade teacher, Lura Sewick, unquestionably had a significant and lasting effect on my life. She taught me the "3 R's" of good government: rights, respect, and responsibility. The simple, yet powerful, ways she taught about government and citizenship inspired me to public service. Without someone like Lura Sewick, I doubt if I would be Governor today.

Jeff Bridges
Actor

I remember Mr. Walrachee. Every time the class did exceptionally well on a test he would swallow a raw egg or one of his many inventions that he claimed were non-toxic. I particularly remember him drinking an entire bottle of adhesive, meant to hold up hosiery. He was a wacky – wonderful guy!

Marjorie Brody
Communications Coach, Author
President, Brody Communications, LTD.

I was a floundering tenth grade student who was very talkative and exuberant. My speech teacher thought he could channel my energy in a more positive way, and got me into speech communications classes and drama courses.

Now I am a successful professional speaker, trainer, consultant and author who is working on her eight and ninth books.

Needless to say, I consider this teacher to be my first mentor! His name is Jim Nix.

Kix Brooks
Country Singer, *Brooks & Dunn*

When I entered high school I was at an all time low in my life. Like a lot of young people I wasn't seeing eye to eye with my parents and I was very short on self esteem. I didn't realize it at the time but I had several high school teachers who basically put me on the road to success.

Bob Wood is a prime example. I never was very good in math. My previous teachers had always said, "He's very bright, if he would only apply himself". Truth was, I just didn't get it. Coach Wood, (he also coached basketball), took the time to make sure I "got it" and once I did "I rocked". Kids that never gave me the time of day were asking for my help. Tutor sessions turned into real friendships. I went to the state math contest in Geometry and my senior year went to the University to study College Algebra and Trigonometry.

While Coach Wood was teaching me that Math was not some mysterious unobtainable science, I often found myself asking him many "real life" questions and came away with a secure sense of honesty, integrity and the right way to handle many different confrontations. It wouldn't have mattered what business I pursued in life, these lessons and this confidence was a much needed commodity. My life would surely have been much different without the influence of my high school teachers.

Helen Gurley Brown
Editor-in-Chief, International Editions, *Cosmopolitan*

Mrs. Oates at Pulaski Heights Grammar School in Little Rock, Arkansas, was my first teacher. I was six years old. She told my mother I had special performing talent. She made me Mother Goose in the class play and I was the star whereas Jack and the Beanstalk and Little Miss Muffett, Jack Spratt and others only reported to me. I was in every scene! I went on writing and performing in little grammar school and junior high projects from that moment. In senior high, a really splendid English teacher— mousy, ancient (she must have been all of 50), not popular with other students, thought I had a little writing ability, but more than that, she thought that everybody should learn the rules of grammar and appreciate good writing. Ms. Ethel McGee helped me with the performing arts when I entered a debating contest. She coached me all the way through my valedictory address graduation night. My mother was a school teacher and she helped too. What interests me is that these women were "mousy" but they got it out of others!

Carol M. Browner
Former Administrator / U.S. Environmental Protection Agency

While growing up in Southern Florida, my parents were my most influential teachers, instilling in me a deep-seeded passion and appreciation for learning and for the natural world. My parents also taught me the importance of giving back to my community through pursuing a career in public service or working in the community to make our world a better place to live.

My father, an Irish immigrant and a high school dropout, came to the United States, completed his high school education and put himself through college. My mother, who also grew up in Ireland, taught me the importance of Irish culture and my heritage. Both of my parents not only became respected professors at Miami-Dade Community College, but they also raised three daughters and sent all of us to college.

With the guidance and support of my parents, I chose to give back to my community by working to ensure clean air, healthy water and safe land for all Americans. My parents were the driving force in my life and provided me with the tools necessary to understand my environment, community, and world.

Dave Brubeck
Jazz Musician

There have been several teachers who have made a difference in my life. The first one was a high school teacher who surprised me by telling me that I was "college material." In my own mind I did not even consider going to college. I intended to stay on my father's ranch and become a cattle rancher. I had a mother who had ambitions for me. She insisted that I follow in my two older brothers' footsteps and go to college, so an agreement was made that I would study to be a veterinarian at the College of the Pacific in Stockton, California and then return to the cattle ranch.

I was taking the typical Freshman pre-med course that included such subjects as chemistry and zoology, and not progressing well, when one day, Dr. Arnold, the zoology teacher, said to me, "Brubeck, your mind is not on dissecting frogs and the various experiments we're doing in the lab. You are always listening to the music coming across the lawn from the music conservatory. Why don't you just go over there next year?" I did. This move definitely changed the course of my life.

Within the conservatory I found another teacher, who understood me better than I understood myself, J. Russell Bodley. He encouraged me as a composer and as a jazz musician and seemed to find in me a raw talent that I didn't know I possessed. He continued to be involved with my career and my music to the end of his life. And, even now when I am past eighty years old, I often return to that conservatory, which in many ways I never left.

The archives from my long career in music are now preserved in the library of that university, and an institute for gifted musicians has been established in my name at the University of the Pacific. I am hoping that the teachers these young people will meet will make the difference in their lives that Dr. Arnold and Dr. Bodley made in mine.

Red Buttons
Comedian, Actor

My soccer coach "Bill" Weinstein at Evander Childs High School in the Bronx said to the team when we lost the championship game to James Monroe High School "Winning or losing doesn't build character - doing the best you can does" - I've lived with that.

Ruth Buzzi
Comedienne

Mrs. Helen King, my dance teacher from 7 to 13 years old had the biggest effect on my life. Why? I probably was the worst student in our small dance class. My dad would ask me from time to time if I was having fun in the classes, so I took that to mean I wouldn't (and didn't) have to practice between lessons...hence... I was the worst, because the other students did practice.

Each week, Miss King taught us a new step. I almost always (unless it looked easy) let the others "go first". We'd have to do it alone in front of Helen, then in front of our mothers. Every time I knew the rest were doing it better than I would, (which was very often as the years rolled on), I would do the new step as well as I could for Miss King, but, out of embarrassment, FUNNY in front of our mothers. To hear them laugh was a wonderful relief!!!

By the time we all reached out eighth grade year, Miss King approached me and asked if I would be willing to let her teach me a funny ballet she knew for our annual dance recital. She said

34

the other girls would do the ballet correctly, but I would do it incorrectly. I was *Thrilled* with the idea!!!

The ballet was the biggest hit of the recital and I got my first taste of making 500 people laugh at once… many times. Need I say more!!!

Fran Capo
Comedienne, *World's Fastest Talking Woman*

Two teachers stick out in my mind the most, my fifth grade teacher Mrs. Williams and my mom, Rose who is a preschool teacher in Queens.

When I was in fifth grade I decided I wanted to write a book and get it published. I came up with this crazy book called "Jupiee from Jupiter". To make the book funny I pasted in Bazooka Joe comic strips from the bubble gum I collected. Of course at the time I had no knowledge of copyright infringements. Anyway, I pulled Mrs. Williams on the side and asked her to look at my "masterpiece." She took it home and read it. The next day, she wrote me a lovely note telling me that the book was funny and she looked forward to seeing my name in print someday. Looking back, the book was really bad, but the spark she set off stayed with me. She could have easily discouraged me, (and corrected the dozens of spelling mistakes) but instead she let me have my dream. So far, I have published three books and many freelance articles. I don't know where Mrs. Williams is today, but I sure hope she got to see my name in print and realize that she was a factor in my success.

Dreams can easily be crushed or nurtured and it takes a special kind of teacher to realize the power they can have on young minds. My mom Rose instills that power in her students. My mother is one of the most positive and loving teachers I have ever seen. When I pick her up from school there are always a dozen kids clinging to her, yelling Mrs. Rose. Kids have named their pets and computers after her. She is invited to the children's soccer ball games and birthday parties. Besides teaching the kids the basic skills, she also teaches them what she taught me, "That Nothing is Impossible." That is a lesson that stays with you for life.

I thank them both.

Arne H. Carlson
Former Governor, Minnesota

Special teachers don't just teach their students, they expose their students to creative and expansive ideas. They create connections between what and how students live and learn. Special teachers make learning fun and interesting, while encouraging their students to reach for even higher goals. Unique teachers don't simply encourage and inspire their students for a moment in time, they walk beside them through their lives, becoming inspirations to pass the gift of knowledge with the joy of learning on to others. Special teachers go the extra mile and I was fortunate to have many fine teachers.

Mel Carnahan
Former Governor, Missouri

My favorite teacher was my seventh grade social studies teacher, Colon Ritter. He taught at Kramer Jr. High in Washington, D.C. Mr. Ritter was a key figure in my life. He helped encourage my interest in politics and current affairs.

Thomas R. Carper
Governor, Delaware

I still correspond with my dear first grade teacher, Mrs. Anderson, at least once a year. She got me started with all the basics—reading, writing and arithmetic—in a combined class of first and second graders. I credit a great deal of my success today to the solid foundation Mrs. Anderson helped me build.

Jimmy Carter
39th President of the United States, Author, Social Activist, 2002 Nobel Peace Prize Winner

Miss Julia Coleman was the school superintendent and my teacher when I was a child, and she greatly influenced my life. She taught all of her students to seek cultural knowledge beyond the requirements of the normal rural school classroom. As a schoolboy who lived in an isolated farm community, my exposure to classical literature, art and music was insured by this superlative teacher. I will always be grateful for all she taught me.

Fr. Brian Cavanaugh
Holy Spirit Friary, Franciscan University

The one teacher that stands out in my memory is Fr. Carl Starkloff, SJ. I was in my 4th year of grad school for my Master's in Divinity degree taking a class at Regis College in Toronto, Canada. What I remember so distinctly is that Fr. Carl graded with *green* pens, not red; and he told you what was correct, rather than pointing out just what was wrong. For example, "Karl Rahner says something very similar to this, but you need to develop your idea further." He could have said, "That's an incomplete thought."

Fr. Carl gave you hope rather than crush the spirit. Just look at the color green. It's a sign of verdant life, spring, go lights, hope; while red signifies errors, stop signs, danger, warning. Sure it's a subtle message but 14 years later it stands out in my memory.

Benjamin J. Cayetano
Governor, Hawaii

There is not one teacher specifically that I could pick out—there were so many who had a positive impact on my life. Since my father was a single parent who worked long hours, I often times turned to my school teachers for support and guidance. My teachers became my role models. In them, I found encouragement and hope, which continues to inspire me today.

Bob Chase
President, National Education Association

For me, that special teacher is Alan Carlsen, my high school English teacher and track coach at Dennis-Yarmouth Regional High School in South Yarmouth, Mass. Alan Carlsen opened up a lot of things for me. He made me realize I had something to offer, and provided me with the opportunity to develop my self-confidence. I recall that Carlsen had the ability to let students know each was important, and not just someone in the classroom. There was never a question in my mind that he cared.

Lawton Chiles
Former Governor, Florida

I believe it was Mrs. Tilly from Lake Morton Grammar School (Lakeland, Florida) who stands out most in my mind. She was my fifth grade teacher. Mrs. Tilly was pretty important to me because I was always getting into trouble. She was always encouraging me to keep on "keeping on" – not to get discouraged. You might say she believed in tough love, but she was also very supportive. She said I had what it took to be a success, but I needed to buckle down and tough it out.

Eleanor Clift
Contributing Editor, *Newsweek*

I am delighted to participate in any project that honors teachers.

Yes, I have had special teachers. The one I remember most vividly is Mr. Bohan. He was my sixth grade teacher at P.S. 152 in Queens, and the first male teacher I ever had. This was the 1950's. Elementary schools were female ghettos in those days. Mr. Bohan would have stood out even if he had been a terrible teacher. And he was great. I flourished under his attention. It sounds terribly sexist to admit this today, but a male teacher was so unusual then that everything we did in his classroom took on added value. Remember, this was the era where child-raising was not considered a manly activity, and many men, including my father, had little to do with their grade-school children. With Mr. Bohan's encouragement, I took a test that qualified me for an accelerated program in junior high school, where I did three years in two, skipping eighth grade. I'm not sure of his first name—William comes to mind. I think he went on to become a principal of P.S. 152, but I could be making that up. Mr. Bohan was big like a football player, and Irish-looking. I know that because I still have the pictures from our sixth-grade trip to Central Park.

Jeff Cook
Vocals, lead guitar, fiddle for *Alabama*

One of my dearest and most memorable teachers was Mary Ann Horton-Lurie. She was my Senior English Teacher. This was her first full year of teaching since graduating from college. Perhaps, because she was closer to our age, she was better able to communicate with the Seniors. She seemed more like one of the students than our teacher.

Once, during a classroom discussion, I disagreed with her on a point. She thought for a few minutes then said "You know, you're right." In my 12 years of schooling, she was the only teacher I remember ever admitting being wrong. Her honesty made a lasting impression on me.

She seemed to have a knack for going slightly against the grain with the principal. I don't think I'm the only one who felt that she really cared about us and wanted us to retain what she was teaching.

She was also co-director of the senior play which, of course, meant extra hours in addition to preparing assignments and grading papers. But, even with all the extra work, she seemed to enjoy what she was doing and a certain amount of pride went with each of us who graduated.

We still stay in touch and we laughingly say, "She learned me real good."

Robin Cook, M.D.
Author

I remember my fourth grade teacher, Mrs. Korth, whom I believe was responsible for awakening my interest in academics. I know competition is currently in disfavor, but Mrs. Korth made a chart on the wall with all the kids' names. Next to each name was a plastic airplane on a thumb tack. If a student got 100 on the weekly spelling test, his (or her) plane would move out one box on the graph-like chart. Responding to this stimulus, my plane began to soar as my spelling tests went from miserable to 100! And along with my spelling came everything else.

Thank you Mrs. Korth!

Denton Cooley, M.D.
Renowned Heart Surgeon

Personally, I believe nothing is more important in our society than proper understanding of the English language. Therefore, I will mention the name of an English teacher from the eighth grade at Sidney Lanier Junior School in Houston. Her name was Mrs. Weinheimer.

Mrs. Weinheimer influenced my education in a most important way. She drilled English grammar into the students in almost military fashion. Her insistence on the ability to diagram sentences so that we would know not only the parts, but the essential elements of grammar and composition. Throughout my life, I have felt grateful for her efforts in this regard, believing this has prepared me in the fundamentals of life as a teacher myself and as a citizen.

Roger Cossack
Journalist, CNN

I'm afraid that I was not much of a student. Oh, I got pretty good grades because I excelled in taking exams, but really not learning very much.

However, I was somehow able to get into UCLA Law School. I went not because I felt a strong calling to the law, but because I really couldn't figure out what else to do. The only thing I was good at was going to school.

However, during my first year I took a course in Constitutional Law from Professor Ken Karsh. It was as if an explosion took place in my head. I eagerly waited for his class and could hardly wait for him to trace the history of the court and its influence on our law and culture. I knew that I had made the right decision with my life and Professor Karsh was and is my inspiration. We are still friends today.

41

Michael Crichton, M.D.
Author

I had lots of good teachers that I still remember vividly, starting with Miss Fromkin in the third grade, who first encouraged me in writing. Later Miss Bennett and Mr. McGrath both read my writing in high school. I churned out lots of pages in those days, and most of it was pretty awful—I don't know how they could read all that, week after week, but I'm grateful they did. I'm still in contact with Mr. McGrath, and saw Miss Bennett a couple of years ago, when I visited my old high school.

But I'm one of those people who was unbelievably lucky in my teachers. I had wonderful teachers in nearly all subjects, all through my school years, and still remember them very well. From time to time, I drift off and find myself thinking about Mr. Rex, my seventh grade teacher; Miss Clark, my amazing Latin teacher; Miss Pataki, my Biology teacher... I was just very lucky.

Judith Crist
Author

I would like to pay tribute to three teachers who made a mark on my life.

First, there was Louis K. Wechsler, my eighth-term English teacher at Morris High School in the Bronx in New York City in the spring of 1937. Beyond the curriculum, which included my introduction to *Hamlet*, he taught me that the correct name of that institution was Johns Hopkins and that an "educated" person should know Latin, Greek, and Hebrew. I wound up with a passion for the first and, alas, only smatterings of the latter two, but oh, that passion for Latin! And he sent me as a delegate from our "literary" magazine to the Scholastic Press Conference where I not only saw and heard in person our then First Lady, Eleanor

Roosevelt, wonder of wonders, but shook hands with her at the "banquet" luncheon—a touch of greatness.

Second, was Vere L. Rubel, an English professor at Hunter College, who introduced me to *Middlemarch* and the other great works and became a personal friend for the rest of her life. Most memorably, when I wrote to her about the unresponsiveness of freshman-English students I encountered out west in the course of a fellowship, she replied, "If you make a mark on one student out of a hundred, you can consider yourself a successful teacher." Her encouragement was essential to my ultimate dedication not only to journalism as reporter and then critic but also to teaching itself for the past 40 years on the part-time faculty of the Graduate School of Journalism of Columbia University.

The third major influence of my life was Hoxie Neal Fairchild, a professor in English at Hunter College who was my "honors" course professor in my senior year. The climax of the course was a "learned, scholarly dissertation" of the student's choice. My final paper was *Tom Jones Goes to Vanity Fair: A Comparative Study of Henry Fielding and William M. Thackeray*. I had a wonderful time doing the paper about two still-favorite satirical novelists but it wound up being more readable than scholarly. Said H. N. Fairchild: "Some there are who write for the *PMLA* (the *Publication of the Modern Language Association*) and some there are who write for the *New Yorker*—and believe me, my dear, there's no shame in writing for *The New Yorker*." Suffice it that two years after graduation I gave up my attempts at the scholarly life (I'd begun graduate work on 18th-century English lit.)—and though I've never, so far, written for *The New Yorker*, I have written for newspapers, magazines, television, and radio and other mass media, including cyberspace. My thanks to the teacher who taught me who I was not.

Walter Cronkite
Journalist

Life and the course we take through it are affected by many circumstances, some beneficial, some considerably less so. This is an observation that is unlikely to be quoted in any compendium of great philosophical thought. Others have even remarked on the fact before me.

But I am inclined to these lofty terms when I think of those events that followed upon meeting Fred Birney, a rather slight man of unprepossessing mien who, despite his glasses, always wore a frown, as if he were looking for something beyond the range of his sight. He was an inspired teacher who directed the course of my life. He wasn't even a professional teacher, but he had the gift.

Fred Birney was a newspaperman who thought that high schools ought to have courses in journalism. That was a highly innovative idea at the time, but by presenting himself as an unpaid volunteer and the program as a virtual no-cost item, he convinced the Houston School Board. He spent a couple of days each week circulating among Houston's five high schools preaching the fundamentals of a craft he loved.

His arrival on the scene at San Jacinto was timed as if decreed in heaven. That same year, suffering the disabling shin splints that kept me off the track team and realizing that I'd never make the football team at 110 pounds (and with distinctly limited talent), I had wrangled the job of sports editor of the *Campus Cub*, our semi-occasional school paper.

Adding to the happy confluence of events, I had just read an exciting short story in *American Boy* magazine. That publication was printing a series of fiction pieces featuring various occupations, a little push toward career guidance. None intrigued me as much as that on the newspaperman.

With my interest thus already piqued, I was a sitting duck for Fred Birney, missionary from the Fourth Estate. I sat enthralled as this wiry man, this bundle of energy, sat on the edge of the classroom desk spinning tales from the world of print. I devoured not only every book he assigned but every one on journalism and journalists that I could find in the library. This turned out to stand me in good stead.

That year he entered me in the newswriting competition of the Texas Interscholastic Press Association. We finalists sat at typewriters as a set of facts was printed on the blackboard. From them we were to write our thousand-word stories. The facts that were presented were from the notorious Leopold-Loeb murder case, in which two brilliant young scions of Chicago's wealthiest, most socially prominent families kidnapped and murdered fourteen-year-old Bobby Franks, another boy from their set.

The Chicago *Daily News* report on the case had become an entry in the 1924 edition of an annual compilation of the year's best news stories. Purely by happenstance, with no thought of preparing for the contest, I had just read that very story the night before. My competition didn't have a chance as I loaded my entry with descriptive matter that must have amazed, and puzzled, the judges. Always a fast typist since taking a junior high school course in the art, I ripped the last page out of my machine and delivered the completed story to the front of the room while most of the others were struggling with their leads. I won.

I take a certain pride in having maintained a reputation for fast copy throughout my newspaper career. Fast-breaking stories left my typewriter in a hurry. Not great literature, perhaps, but fast, and usually accurate.

I wasn't the only one in our class to catch Fred Birney's eye. Bill Bell would develop into a superb newspaperman, and David

Westheimer would go on to Hollywood to write such classics as *Von Ryan's Express* and *Watching Out for Dulie.*

The next year I was editor of the *Campus Cub.* Birney put its publication on a regular schedule so we would learn something about editing against a deadline, and he took us to the printer's to teach us makeup and composing room skills.

We were a small group, we student journalists, and maybe that was the secret of Birney's success. But I felt that those spectacles of his were magnifying for him every move I made. I suppose my colleagues felt the same. He led us through our copy, showing us how to tighten here, explain more there, use adjectives and adverbs with caution lest they imply editorial opinion. He suggested questions we might have asked our interview subjects, noted facts we might have developed to improve our report. And every criticism, every suggestion, made clear that there was sacred covenant between newspaper people and their readers. We journalists had to be right and we had to be fair.

I had a sense whenever I was in his presence that he was ordering me to don my armor and buckle on my sword to ride forth in a never-ending crusade for the truth. Good journalism, journalism that would please Fred Birney, became our Holy Grail. He so inspired us that Charlie Dyer and I, unable to get our fill of journalism, even started what surely must have been one of the country's early unofficial high school newspapers, even before the term "underground" was used. We put out four mimeographed pages that we called *The Reflector.* It could not be called lofty. In fact, it was a scandal sheet, filled with probably libelous comments on the doings of San Jacinto school society. On occasion it also dipped into the doings of the school administration. It turned out that its publishers had more gall than courage, and in the face of some rather specific threats to their life and limb, they wisely folded the paper after a few editions.

Birney applauded our enterprise. He frowned at our tabloid style.

Birney as far as I know, was never taught to teach. His strength was his deep practical knowledge of his subject, his love of it, and his intense desire to communicate that knowledge and that love to others. That must be the secret of all great teachers, and the shame is that there are probably thousands of them out there who are denied a chance to practice that talent because of crowded facilities, disciplinary overload and stultifying work rules imposed by bureaucratic administrations and selfish unions.

Dick DeVos
President, Amway Corporation

One of my teachers at Grand Rapids Christian High School was Dr. Leonard Greenway. My grades were not very good, but I managed to get through school. When I graduated, Dr. Greenway wrote a simple sentence in my yearbook. That message is an example of the power teachers have every day. To this student who didn't appear destined to be powerful or on anyone's honor roll, Dr. Greenway wrote this simple line, "With talents for leadership in God's kingdom."

I looked at those words and wondered what he really meant by them, because I'd never thought of myself in those terms. In later years, I marveled at his wisdom, because he understood what a few written words from a highly respected Bible teacher would one day mean to me. He came to our high school class's fortieth reunion where I happened to be the Emcee, and I was about to remind him of what he'd written. He stopped me and said, "You don't have to tell me what I wrote. I know what I wrote in your yearbook 40 years ago." Then he quoted the line to me. And I've often wondered since if he wrote that in every yearbook. Maybe he did, but it doesn't matter, because his words inspired me to try to live up to them.

Mike Ditka
Former NFL Coach (Chicago Bears, New Orleans Saints), Sport Commentator

The best teacher I had in high school was Mr. Aschman, and he taught history. Mr. Aschman was also the football coach, and it was interesting to see how similar he was in teaching history and football.

He was a man of great character and value and he set a great example for all of us students and athletes.

Elizabeth Dole
Former President, American Red Cross; Former U.S. Secretary of Transportation

I was extremely fortunate to feel the beneficial influence of many excellent teachers during elementary school, high school, college and graduate schools. It wouldn't be possible for me to mention just one teacher of mine. However, I do recall hearing the following:

A wise teacher once advised her class:

"Spend every possible hour in your library
for there you will find windows to the entire world."

Robert Dole
Former Senator (Kansas), Former Presidential Candidate

My hometown of Russell, Kansas has a fine record of preparing young people for a rich and fulfilling life. There are many outstanding mentors and educators who devoted all that they had to helping young people.

I recall one of many, Coach Harold Elliot. Whether on the basketball court or in the classroom, he brought out the best in each of us. He was a caring person who had a teacher's talent for instilling confidence and cultivating skills.

Vincent J. Dooley
Director of Athletics, University of Georgia

As a student in grammar school, high school, college, in the Marines, in graduate school, and as a part-time student auditing college courses, it has been my experience that there are common threads among all of the memorable teachers that I have ever had. They all had a passion for their subject which was reflected in their enthusiasm, and they were all demanding but yet willing to spend time with each students who had a thirst for knowledge.

That was true of Sister Patricia, a nun who taught me in the fourth grade in grammar school. It was true of Brother Max my religious teacher at a Catholic high school as well as my high school coach, Ray Dicharry. It was true of my English teacher at Auburn University, Ms. Frances McCloud. It was true of a Marine officer whose name I can't recall who grabbed my attention as a lecturer in basic school. It was true of Graham Collier who taught art history at the University of Georgia, and it is currently true of Drs. Michael Dirr and Allan Armitage, two University professors who taught horticulture courses I have recently audited at the University.

All of these individuals and several others along the way have stimulated in me a great quest for learning and perhaps that is what teaching is all about.

Richard Dreyfuss
Actor

Gladys Wilcox was a teacher of mine at Horace Mann Elementary School. She was a humorless, impatient, frustrating, bitter, rotten human being.

And after I left school, after I left her class, I never thought about her again. And about 20 years later, I was having a conversation with a friend of mine, and we were reminiscing about elementary school, and all of a sudden in that conversation, it occurred to me that many of the things that I had come to love in my life, Shakespeare, history, reading literature, all had come out of this woman's class.

And I was struck by the fact that she had, you know, not liked me very much and not seemed to encourage me very much, but she got the job done.

And so I tracked her down. I found her in a retirement home in southern California. I called her up. She answered the phone, and I said, "Mrs. Wilcox, you won't remember me. My name is Richard Dreyfuss. I was a student of yours at Horace Mann Elementary, and I just want you to know that many of the things I've come to love in my life I learned in your class." And she said, "Thank you very much," and hung up.

There's a point to that story, but I also had a teacher by the name of Rose Jane Landau – may she rest in peace – who taught a class in drama when I was a teenager. She happened to gather together a greater collection of neurotic, misfit, outcast children than have ever been brought together in one place at any one time; and she was also, like Gladys Wilcox, a great teacher. She was great because she allowed us to believe that we were, in fact, as talented as we thought we were.

And those two people were not the only great teachers I had, but they kind of represent two areas, two polar opposites that lead to great teaching and grateful students. And wherever they are, I thank them.

Mort Drucker
Cartoonist-*Mad* Magazine

When I was seven years old, my elementary teacher, a young woman, gave me a sealed note to bring home to my parents. I could not imagine what I had done to inspire that note. My teacher thought I had, at that age, unusual talent in art and suggested that my parents encourage me to continue drawing and enroll me in art classes to further my talent.

I regret having lost track of this wonderful teacher who took a special interest in me. I firmly believe teachers are the most important professionals as they influence and inspire each generation of young students.

Michael S. Dukakis
Former Governor, Massachusetts, Former Presidential Candidate

I started with a great role model – my mother, who came to this country from Greece when she was nine, was one of the first Greek girls ever to go to college in the U.S., taught school for four years before she married my dad, and is still going strong at the age of 95!

But, like all of us, I had some great and inspiring teachers. One of the best was Kate O'Brien, my high school French teacher and the head of the Modern Foreign Languages Department at Brookline High School when Kitty and I were students there. She was a great woman and a fantastic teacher. She gave me a love of languages and an appreciation for other cultures that I have had ever since. Shortly before her death and before I decided to run for the Presidency, she bequeathed a thousand dollars in her will to my campaign committee in the event that I decided to run for the presidency. It was the first contribution to my presidential campaign. How can you not be inspired by teachers like that?

Ralph Edwards
Entertainer, Game Show Pioneer

My elementary teacher in Merino, Colorado, who had the greatest influence in my career was Miss Effie Anderson. Miss Effie inspired and encouraged me to set my goals in life. She cared about her students' well-being and was always there to help us obtain our vision in life.

My college professors who encouraged me further in drama were Professors Charles Von Neumayer and Sarah Huntsman Sturgess from the University of California, Berkeley. Professor Neumayer said to me: "Even if you have to crawl to New York, you must do so."

I am truly grateful to my teachers who taught me to create situations beyond the small scope of my world. One teacher who will enlarge the world for her students can outdo anything written on paper.

Michael Eisner
Chief Executive Officer of The Walt Disney Company

What inspired me most about a teacher I had named Bruce McClellan was his passion for excellence, long before excellence became a buzzword in best-selling books.

Bruce's point was that if you were going to write an English paper, you should write the greatest English paper possible . . . and if you were going to play soccer, you should play soccer at the highest possible level, and if you were going to make your bed, you should do the best possible job at that.

High standards should apply to every sphere in your life, he told us, though not everything you did carried equal weight or importance. The message stuck with me. When I found myself programming afternoon soap operas at ABC, I made it my goal to produce the best possible soap operas, and I didn't wring my hands that I wasn't making *Long Day's Journey into Night.*

I remember Dr. Consolo as a great character who stood up on the table to lecture, played the trumpet in class, recited poetry and was utterly passionate about words and literature.

Each of these men fueled my later interest in dramas built around teachers. At ABC, I got involved in "Room 222" and "Welcome Back Kotter," the show that launched John Travolta's career.

Early on at Disney, during an ideas meeting, one of our executives mentioned a script titled *Dead Poets Society* about a passionate poetry professor. I responded instinctively to the idea, and thought immediately of Dr. Consolo. Virtually everyone else thought that a movie in which language was the star would never fly at the box office. But I insisted on pursuing it, and *Dead Poets Society* proved to be one of the two or three best movies we have yet made at Disney, as well as a great commercial success.

Other more recent teacher-centered Disney movies have been *Dangerous Minds* and *Mr. Holland's Opus*, both of which were also resounding successes at the box office.

William C.(Bill) Elliott
NASCAR Driver, Winston Cup Champion

As the parent of three children education is of the utmost importance in my family's life. Dedicated teachers, such as yourself, are often overlooked as the key to our future. As to my personal experience as a student, it was an English High School teacher that was most influential. She was a kind woman, who required hard work, dedication and motivated students to achieve their goals. Setting standards for students and doing whatever it took to achieve these goals was her primary aspiration. Her "No Negative" approach to teaching, taught me that if you remain positive and focused on your dreams they come true. For the last 25 years my dream of becoming a NASCAR Winston Cup driver has come true every morning I wake up. If it were not for her guiding me to follow through with my dreams, I would not be where I am at today. Her motivational teaching taught me that hard work and dedication do prevail.

Joanne Eschrich
Sculptor, Hallmark Ornaments

I had several special teachers during my high school years at Westport High School in Massachusetts, but one teacher who influenced me the most was Mr. Feeney.

Confidence is what my high school teacher Mr. Bill Feeney gave me as a 16 year old "budding" artist. We both had an interest in Scrimshaw (etching into ivory or bone) and after recognizing my artistic talent, he entrusted me with rare and valuable pieces of ivory to carve. With this kind of material, there is no room for error, no second chance. I remember being struck by the confidence that this person had in me and my artistic skills. It was then that I realized I had the potential to make a living doing what I loved best... being an artist.

Marsha Johnson Evans
Former National Executive Director, Girl Scouts of America;
President, American Red Cross

My personal development and career journey have been impacted by more than a single teacher, but there is one who stands out in my memory. Her name is Mrs. Alice Dauer. She was an English teacher who also coached the debate and drama clubs at my high school. I had her for English my senior year in high school. I also lived with her during my senior year.

During my junior year, my parents came to me one day with news that we were moving to another part of California. The news was devastating to me. I was a good student and I didn't want to relocate because I knew I had an excellent chance of being the top graduate in my school. My parents always encouraged my academic pursuits and they told me that if I could arrange an appropriate living situation, they would let me stay behind. I did. Mrs. Dauer allowed me to live with her the entire school year. She encouraged me to explore new facets of myself like acting, which I really enjoyed. She also took me to evaluate various colleges and she helped me become more focused in my thinking. It was a rare and generous thing she did for me. Living with Mrs. Dauer that year was a maturing experience that helped me become a confident young woman. At the end of the school term, I graduated as the valedictorian of my class.

Sandra Feldman
President, American Federation of Teachers

When I first went back to visit my high school, long after I had graduated, I was struck by how much smaller the building was than I'd remembered. The second floor hallway, which had housed the English Department, looked too tiny for the enormous worlds that it held for me as a student dreaming of being a great American novelist.

But if the place seemed smaller, the teachers who taught up and down that hallway remain much larger than life. Mr. Coleman, with his intense blue eyes and nicotine stained fingers and gently prodding questions, was my favorite. I found him devastatingly handsome, and I believed he was as painfully sensitive as I myself was. I had heard a rumor that he was the principal writer of Super Boy comics, but I never dared to ask him. Everything we read in his class seemed deeply romantic to me - from Shakespeare to Thomas Hardy. And I was convinced that from his class on, for the rest of my life, literature would sustain me no matter what happened.

I wrote for the school literary magazine, of course, and Mr. Bailin was my editor, agent, and critic. In my yearbook he wrote, "I loved your stories about New York. I know you'll make an impression on it one day." I was always convinced that he was responsible for my getting the Creative Writing award at graduation. Though, alas, my great novel remains unwritten, I still hope to live up to Mr. Bailin's belief in my future.

And last but not least, I vividly remember Miss Horne. Crisp enemy of dangling participles and split infinitives, she gave me confidence in my ability to wield the written word. Did she ever know how many union position papers, picket signs, pithy slogans, and letters to the editor bore her influence? Even after so many years, I can feel the excitement of learning what these great people had to teach me, and my gratitude to them for opening my eyes and my mind is boundless.

Fannie Flagg
Author

My favorite teacher was my sixth grade teacher at Foley Grammar School in Foley, Alabama. I was very shy and she worked very hard at helping me overcome that. She also read "Nancy Drew" to the class and I think it started my love for stories. Her name is Mrs. Sybil Underwood and when I was nominated for an Oscar for my screenplay of *Fried Green Tomatoes*, she was the first person I called!

Ronald Fogelman, General, USAF
Former United States Air Force Chief of Staff

Growing up in a small rural area, many of us never understood why math, especially advanced math skills, would be a subject anyone would ever need or require. In High School, our math teacher, Miss Rearick, was feared by all. She was known as the toughest teacher in the district because she actually made you learn the necessary skills. This could be quite a painful experience for those of us who had no desire to learn the intricacies of algebra, calculus, and trigonometry.

I came to appreciate Miss Rearick and her tough standards when I received an appointment to the United States Air Force Academy. While there, I realized math was one of those subjects that caused the most problems for cadets and was the source of many disenrollments. I had less trouble than most of my fellow cadets getting through these math classes and am convinced Miss Rearick's foresight and teaching discipline was the key to this. Years later, Miss Rearick came to visit my family in Arizona. To my surprise, I found her one Saturday morning watching cartoons with my children. Her love of life and ability to instill the best in everyone has been an inspiration to me and her many students.

Janie Fricke
Country Singer

One of my favorite teachers was Mr. Hal Vizino (still in the Ft. Wayne, Indiana, area) – at the time he taught us French and Choir and his dynamic influence still stays in my mind... he gave me great advice on my singing delivery, and helped me grow as a student.

William German
Editor, *San Francisco Chronicle*

I had the briefest of journalism careers in high school. Within a week of volunteering for the staff of the school weekly, a friend and I were banished for pitching and batting a board eraser with a heavy ruler in the paper's office. Unfortunately the eraser hit and broke a window.

An English teacher, who gave me an A on a term-long book report project added the comment, "You write succinctly." I was puzzled until I looked up the word in the dictionary. Then I was pleased and have tried to write that way ever since.

Do not play baseball with board erasers. Write succinctly.

Nikki Giovanni
Author, Poet

I actually think it my basic nervousness that has always made my handwriting so poor. Well, my handwriting is not poor but it is clearly not the beautiful work of art that others have. My grandfather had a beautiful hand. His letters were perfectly formed with just a touch of flourish to show individuality but not so much that vanity crept in. My grandmother had a serious hand. Her letters bold, clear, one might even say strident. You knew it was from Grandmother from quite a distance away.

Mommy also has a very nice hand with a bit more flourish than Grandpapa, her father. Mommy always likes to break words up with curlicues which I have always admired. But me, well, I never was even good with a pen. There has never been a happier person than when ball point pens became affordable and people like me did not have to suffer through pen and ink.

One of my favorite teachers, if not my very favorite, Miss Alfredda Delaney, always encouraged me in my writing but she would also say You Must Take Typing. You will never be a writer unless you learn to type. At first I was hurt because I couldn't see what typing had to do with creating but I learned. Miss Brice taught typing and the problem with all the skill based subjects is that there is no room for mistakes. I would be extremely discouraged because I was not nearly as fast as a lot of my fellow and sister students. I am still not quick but Miss Delaney would say, "You must stick with it," and because I really did adore Miss Delaney I kept trying.

Mommy gave me an electric typewriter the year I went off to college. Miss Delaney was very proud and extolled again about the importance of typing. I started college typing my papers more because Miss Delaney had convinced me my handwriting was unacceptable than because I believed in the power of typing. I also began rather seriously to write and by cracky! Miss Delaney was right. My grades were better. I know better what I was saying. My papers looked better. And I became a writer. About twenty years later Miss Delaney introduced me at a Writer's Conference with this story. And I am so happy that she was so very right.

John Glenn
Astronaut, Former Senator, Ohio; Former Presidential Candidate

Aside from my parents, who were both readers and instilled in me a love of reading and learning that has served me all my life, the person who was most influential in my life was my high school civics teacher. He demanded the best each student had to offer and had a sensible no-nonsense approach to discipline. He always encouraged students to explore the unknown and try the unfamiliar. He was the one who first made me understand the uniqueness and strengths of our constitutional democracy, and it was under his tutelage that I first developed the determination to participate in national government.

If I am now considered a success it is because I always tried to do my very best at whatever I attempted. I feel being able to succeed comes from being at the right place at the right time with the preparation to take advantage of opportunity. I believe that commitment to ideals, respect for others, and serious study are essential for success in any field.

Jane Goodall
Founder, The Jane Goodall Institute for Wildlife Research, Education and Conservation

When I was a child, I could not spell and I had horrible handwriting. (My spelling is still not too good and people complain bitterly about my writing!) but I *loved* to write – stories, essays, poems. Again and again, I handed in some hard-worked piece, but none of my teachers seemed interested in the ideas or the compositions. Back it came covered in angry red marks where words were misspelled or ill-written. And then I had to write out all the spelling mistakes 10 times each!

Then, when I was in high school, I had a wonderful teacher. I remember her so well-Miss Ludwig. She was not English, but had taken refuge during the second World War. For the very first time, I had a teacher who read what I wrote - who sometimes read it out loud to the class, who gave me good marks and, more importantly, praise. I was inspired to work even harder - and I made a deliberate effort, for the first time, to get my spelling and writing better.

She brought Shakespeare and novels we read—Thomas Hardy and Thackeray - to life. I loved her lessons and I remember her with gratitude to this day. What is so frightening is to wonder how it could have been, during the earlier part of my school life, if I had not had a supportive family at home to listen to my compositions. Wonderful though Miss Ludwig was, would there have been inspiration and passion left in me if my other teachers had only criticized and never encouraged?

Miss Ludwig told my mother I had made her whole teaching career worthwhile. And that was because, under her wise encouragement, my passion for writing grew, developed, and blossomed.

Bob Graham
Former Governor, Florida, United States Senator, Florida

I attended high school at Miami Senior High, graduating in 1955. Eleventh grade history was my favorite subject, and I attribute this to the excellent teaching skills of Mrs. Louise Curry, who made history come alive. Knowledge and appreciation of the past helps as we seek to shape America's future. This history course provided an invaluable foundation for my career in public service.

Rev. Andrew Greeley
Professor, National Opinion Research Center, University of Chicago,
Author, Sociologist, Priest

My favorite high school teacher was a Fr. Thomas Grady, who later went on to be the Bishop of Orlando. Tom was not only a good teacher, but has always been a good friend and he inspired me with a love of literature, especially the writings of people like Francis Thompson, Gerard Manley Hopkins and Joseph Conrad. I'm sure if it hadn't been for him I would never have turned to novel writing.

Bob Greene
Pulitzer Prize Winning Journalist, *Chicago Tribune*

When you're young, and you have yet to have your first successes and failures in the outside world, what a teacher says to you about your abilities in the areas that matter the most to you can have an impact beyond enormous. And what that teacher says does not even have to be said out loud. It can come in a glance.

Mrs. Sara Amos, who taught the journalism class at Bexley High School in Bexley, Ohio, let me know that she thought I could write. Sometimes she told me so—but usually just the expression on her face as she read stories that I'd turn in let me know that she must be thinking I was doing all right. A smile as she reached the end of a paragraph, a slight turn of her head as she read something that I meant to be moving—I knew by watching her that what I was writing was working.

Would my life have taken the direction it has had I not been in her class—or had Bexley not offered a journalism class? I don't know. What I do know is that what got me started was not the prospect of millions of readers spending time with what I wrote—but of one reader, in one classroom, taking a look and letting me see that she thought I should keep doing it. I probably appreciated it then—but not as much as I do now.

Lee Greenwood
Country Singer

My music teacher Fred Cooper, gave me all I needed to become a professional musician throughout my three years in high school. Music theory, dance band, marching band drum major, drum and bugle core, tympani in symphony orchestra, first alto sax in symphony orchestra.

His guidance, and counseling gave me direction, and increased my desire to become successful in my chosen trade. God bless my teacher, Mr. Cooper.

Robert A. Griese
Athlete, Sportscaster

One of the best teachers I ever had was Sister Annette, my fifth grade teacher at Assumption Catholic School in Evansville, Indiana. She was very well liked by all the students, as well as the faculty and staff.

I became very close to her when my father died that year, when I was ten years old. Sister Annette became very close to my mother and the rest of our family, and seemed to take a special interest in me for the rest of the school year, and, in fact, for the rest of my days at Assumption Grade School. She remains a very close friend of my mother's to this day.

Sister Annette was not only a very caring person, but also was very good at teaching skills—and was one of the most popular teachers at my school. How fortunate I was to have her as my teacher, and that particular year!

Winston F. Groom
Author-*Forrest Gump*

University Military School Coach Ed Baker decided one day he was not impressed with my football tackling techniques and ordered me to stay after practice and continuously tackle a big old oak tree, which I did until Coach Baker decided I was not going to knock the thing down. I used the episode in Forrest Gump. It taught me two things, first, that even though some things are impossible, you have to try them anyway and, second, that Coach Baker was an asshole.

I never had Coach Baker for a class but in my senior year I had an English teacher named Stanley Moore who had recently graduated from Harvard. He was not much older than us boys and somehow managed to actually interest us in the plays of Shakespeare, which is no small feat for somebody teaching bozos like us. A small group of us would even go over to his apartment after school sometimes and have a sort of round table literary discussion. I think this was the first time I thought I might actually want to be a writer.

Cathy Guisewite
Cartoonist-"Cathy"

I had two teachers in Junior High who changed my life.

Mr. Brown, a math teacher, reached out to me at my most insecure, confused state, and helped me learn to like and trust myself as I was. His guidance had nothing to do with learning math – he went completely out of his way to take interest in me as a person, and let me feel I had someone to talk to.

Mr. Conarty, a speech teacher, gave me the courage to stand up in front of a group and open my mouth. I've never gone on television or given a speech without reliving being in my Junior High auditorium and hearing his voice cheering me on.

Buddy Hackett
Comedian

8th grade—two sisters, Gertrude Porter and Florence Porter—had a rep for being tough—but I learned so much from them. I interpret their "tuff," as being caring and doing their job! I carry their knowledge to this day.

8th grade—Miss Conway, taught me the three problems of antiquity, fascinating.

5th grade—Miss Browdie was a very fair teacher, of which we saw very little.

Senior year, high school—Miss Edith Kerwin directed me in the school play that year. Naturally I fell in love with her, and never recovered—if you know her, please tell her.

Monty Hall
Entertainer, Game Show Host

In my youth in the city of Winnipeg, Canada, my family was forced to move several times because of economic conditions. Staying in one school for a year and then going to another section of the city made it difficult to form relationships with either students or teachers.

But there is one I remember. Her name was Frances Cheshire. She taught seventh and eighth grade students at Lord Selkirk School. Sensing that I was a fish out of water, she took special pains to make me fit in and enjoy my school year.

About ten years ago I visited my hometown and participated in a three hour phone-call-in show. At one point, the interviewer (having read my autobiography) asked me if I had a favorite teacher. When I answered "Frances Cheshire," he jumped in and said, "Great, because we have Miss Cheshire on the phone right now." We had a five-minute chat, and what pleased me the most was her answer to the host's question "Was Monty your favorite pupil?" She replied – "All my pupils were my favorites!"

Frances Cheshire died at the age of 92.

I shall never forget her.

Marvin Hamlisch
Musician, Composer

At Public School 9 in Manhattan I was precocious, brazen and a nuisance. One day the guidance counselor asked: "Why are you having so much trouble in school? You come from a good home, good parents... so why are you driving everyone nuts?"

"Because nobody lets me play the piano here," I replied.

Thanks to the wise counselor and my sympathetic – and long-suffering – third-grade teacher, Miss Sussman, two custodians soon arrived in our classroom with a Sohmer upright piano.

There were plenty of pianos in my school. In those days, in the early 50's, the arts were an integral part of the curriculum. For music appreciation, you just went to school.

The incomparable Miss Sussman loved the theater. So when our class wanted to put on *H.M.S. Pinafore*, she happily agreed. P.S. 9 had a stage, the kids made a crepe paper ship, and the next thing you knew, we were doing *Pinafore*.

Later I attended the Professional Children's School and Queens College. At Queens I knew that I wanted to be a composer. When I told my mother, she said: "Marvin, I'm sure you'll make a wonderful composer. But if things don't work out, I think you should get a degree in teaching." She added: "Now, do you want a tuna fish sandwich, or some veal cutlets?"

To get my teaching degree, I had to teach an actual class, and was assigned to a tough school in a part of the Upper West Side that I would not normally visit unaccompanied. I had no previous teaching experience, but I set up a record player and brought some albums from home.

I began with the Beatles and explained how a long time ago a guy named Bach wrote the same kind of music. We discussed whether the Beatles were inspired by Bach, or whether they actually stole his stuff or whether they just happened to write like Bach.

Later, I asked the students to bring in music that they enjoyed. They did, and I thought, "I'm starting to feel like a teacher," Soon I suggested we put on a talent show.

The students liked the idea. The show had songs and skits. Each student had a part to play, and knew that his or her role was important. This way the students felt that they, too, were important.

The students also learned each of them depended on the others – that one person's line is another person's cue. They were all in it together. The play made them all partners. So they grew together, succeeded together and enjoyed the applause together.

During our rehearsals, I got to know the students individually, as well as most of their mothers. All except Manuel's mother, who never came to school. "Manuel had discipline problems." But he also had his lines, and was under intense pressure to show up and come through for himself and his classmates. I wasn't sure he would.

"Opening Night" was on a Friday afternoon. These kids, whose dress was an early example of what we now call grunge, arrived in their Sunday Best, and so did their parents. Manuel was terrific. And I finally got to meet his mother.

She was delighted. She explained that Manuel had always been difficult, and belonged to a gang. But with his involvement in music class, she noticed a change. She had watched him rehearse at home with his sisters, and lately he had expressed an interest in acting lessons.

Until then, I thought you had to be talented to put on a show. No! You had to be *motivated.* Maybe then you might discover a talent, if not singing, then perhaps designing the program. I also discovered that a boisterous, petulant, even delinquent child like Manuel, could act. We made these discoveries because we put on a little show.

In the short time I taught, I saw that arts education could help young children feel good, about themselves and about their accomplishments. When they played a new song, or recited new lines, I saw their self-esteem grow, and discovered that personal growth and learning go hand in hand.

A recent report by the President's Committee on the Arts and Humanities finds, "Safe havens of music, theater, dance and visual arts programs have proved particularly potent in stemming violence and drug abuse, and in keeping students from dropping out."

Research shows that arts education is our real stealth weapon against crime, illiteracy and mediocrity. I am now aware of the "b" word – the budget. But I am also aware of the consequences of the "C" word – complacency. Without a strong education in the arts, our entire society shall be poorer and weaker.

Bill Hanna
Animator, Founder, HANNA-BARBERA, INC.

Of all the nice teachers I ever had, my fifth grade teacher Robin Oliver, was my favorite. She had a smile on her face all the time, and was always there to give personal attention to any one of the students that was having a learning problem of any sort whatsoever.

I remember once I had ventured into an area where I was not supposed to venture and was spanked. Robin was called down to witness. I got five swats on my bottom with a belt. I didn't cry, but when I looked up, my teacher Robin was crying, wiping tears from her eyes.

When we were back in class I remember walking up to her desk and kissing her on the cheek and saying, "Don't cry any more Miss Robin. It didn't hurt me and I don't want to hurt you." I remember she smiled, thanked me and sent me back to my desk.

When I got back to my desk, sat down and looked back, she was smiling. Robin kissed her finger and blew the kiss back to my desk.

Jack Hanna
Director Emeritus, Columbus Zoo, Wildlife Expert

The teacher who immediately comes to mind is Mr. Jack Pidgeon, Headmaster of The Kiski Prep School in Saltsburg, PA. I owe a great deal of gratitude to Mr. Pidgeon. He is still Headmaster at Kiski, as he was when I attended from 1963 to 1965. When I was 16 years old, Mr. Pidgeon told me, "At Kiski, a boy does not distinguish himself with his car, his date, or his clothes, but by the way he acts and what he does by his own efforts."

Obviously, in the 1960's, a career in the zoological field was not sought after by many people. Mr. Pidgeon could have easily discouraged me from pursuing this goal. However, Mr. Pidgeon instilled in all of the young men at Kiski that the only way to achieve success, no matter what your goal, is **HARD WORK**. Therefore, I attribute much of my success to the fact that I was taught, at a very young age, that hard work and enthusiasm are the keys to being successful.

I am still in touch with Mr. Pidgeon, and the values that he taught me will remain with me forever. I was blessed with three daughters, but did not have any sons to enroll at Kiski. Maybe one day I will have a grandson who will be able to carry on the Kiski tradition for my family.

Jean Harper
Pilot-Boeing 737 Captain for United Airlines

In my senior year of high school, my English teacher was a Mrs. Dorothy Slaton. Mrs. Slaton was an uncompromising, demanding teacher with high standards and a low tolerance for excuses. She refused to treat her students like children, instead expecting them to behave like the responsible adults they would have to be to succeed in the real world after graduation. I was scared of her at first but grew to respect her firmness and fairness.

One day Mrs. Slaton gave the class an assignment. "What do you think you'll be doing 10 years from now?" I thought about the assignment. Pilot? No way. Flight attendant? I'm not pretty enough-they'd never accept me. Wife? What guy would want me? Waitress? I could do that. That felt safe, so I wrote it down.

Mrs. Slaton collected the papers and nothing more was said. Two weeks later, the teacher handed back the assignments, face down on each desk, and asked this question: "If you had unlimited finances, unlimited access to the finest schools, unlimited talents and abilities, what would you do?" I felt a rush of the old enthusiasm, and with excitement I wrote down all my old dreams. When the students stopped writing, the teacher asked, "How many students wrote the same thing on both sides of the paper?" Not one hand went up.

The next thing that Mrs. Slaton said changed the course of my life. The teacher leaned forward over my desk and said, "I have a little secret for you all. You do have unlimited abilities and talents. You do have access to the finest schools, and you can arrange unlimited finances if you want something badly enough. This is it! When you leave school, if you don't go for your dreams, no one will do it for you. You can have what you want if you want it enough."

The hurt and fears of years of discouragement crumbled in the face of the truth of what Mrs. Slaton had said. I felt exhilarated and a little scared. I stayed after class and went up to the teacher's desk. I thanked Mrs. Slaton and told her about my dream of becoming a pilot. Mrs. Slaton half rose and slapped the desk top. "Then do it!" she said.

So I did. It didn't happen overnight. It took 10 years of hard work, facing opposition that ranged from quiet skepticism to outright hostility. It wasn't in my nature to stand up for myself when someone refused or humiliated me; instead, I would quietly try to find another way.

I became a private pilot and then got the necessary ratings to fly air freight and even commuter planes, but always as a copilot. My employers were openly hesitant about promoting me-because I was a woman. Even my father advised me to try something else. "It's impossible," he said. "Stop banging your head against the wall!"

But I answered, "Dad, I disagree. I believe that things are going to change, and I want to be at the head of the pack when they do."

In 1978, I became one of the first three female pilot trainees ever accepted by United Airlines and one of only 50 women airline pilots in the nation at the time. Today, I am a Boeing 737 Captain for United.

It was the power of one well-placed positive word, one spark of encouragement from a woman I respected, that gave that uncertain young girl the strength and faith to pursue her dream. I chose to believe her.

Barbara Harris
Editor-in-Chief, *Shape*

I had many teachers who were influential during my school days, including high school and college:

I remember Sharon Godwin, who introduced herself as, "Hi, I'm Mrs. Godwin. You can call me God for short." I remember her not only for her humor but because of her passion for world literature. She made Dante's *Inferno* and the *Iliad* and the *Odyssey* larger than life and so inviting. She made the characters and the whole subject come to life.

Alice Gay was my physical education teacher in high school and coach for various teams, including volleyball, softball, and basketball. She always expected the best from us, both supporting and pushing us in her class, on the playing field and beyond. She was interested in how we performed in classes beyond her tutelage and helped us to weave our future by listening to us and guiding our dreams and aspirations. Her love for teaching and coaching were obvious and palpable, and the effects of her intense interest in the well-being of her students was unforgettable to myself and many of my team/classmates. In fact, I chose to pursue teaching, to affect the lives of other youngsters like myself, because of her significant influence on my life. She was a teacher and a wonderful life guide.

Orrin Hatch
United States Senator, Utah

My high school years were spent in Pittsburgh, Pennsylvania, at Baldwin High School. I had many great teachers and wonderful memories of my school days. One of my English teachers, Eleanor Smith, had a great influence on me and could perhaps be my favorite. She gave me a love for English literature which has been with me all my life. Among other things, she was able to get across the idea of lifelong learning. I have kept in touch with her for years and have always been thankful for her wisdom and caring.

Heloise
Newspaper Columnist/Household Hints

I was blessed to have some wonderful teachers through my school years, but two stand out in my mind in particular.

Mrs. Ruth Day, who while I was attending Gunston Junior High School 1964-1966, taught mathematics. She didn't so much as "teach" to us, she showed us how wonderful and interesting math could be. When I moved with my family in 1966, I told her that I had to go to Texas and would miss her. To this day I can see her at the blackboard, chalk in hand, moving down the board, explaining $f(x)$ to me, knowing I would pick it up quickly and take it with me. P.S. I did!

From 1969-1974 as a college student at Southwest Texas State University I was blessed to have Dr. Henry McEwen as a professor for several classes over the years. Many times I was the only, or one of few girls in some advanced math classes. It could have been dicey, but because Dr. McEwen didn't treat us any differently, it was just straight math! Well, he made it understandably fun and always challenging. He also made us laugh with the stories of his hogs and farm animals, and could we use calculus to help him design a hog trough? We did!

I still have a funky, purple knit hat that was my favorite during those "Hippy" times, and every time I pull it out, I think of him teasing me about borrowing it to slop hogs!

My heartfilled thanks to all teachers who go the extra mile. Who take a little more time than they have for the student who needs it and who will walk right into heaven with the best hall pass of all! Our thanks!

Arthur Hiller
Movie Director

Eva Howard, my high school drama teacher in Edmonton, Alberta, Canada taught me so much, not just about drama and how it opens questions of life and society, but the values of learning, the values of caring... and not just to see and understand problems, but to get in there and do something about them.

Also, through her support, I was offered a Drama Scholarship to Ohio State University. I turned it down, despite my love of theater, because I thought, "That's not how you earn a living...that's what you do on weekends." Her instincts were right. For the past forty-seven years I've been a director – first in radio, then live TV, then film TV and then movies. I love it and I love and cherish her for her faith and leadership... and what a lovely, warm lady.

Tara Dawn Holland
Miss America 1997

Alice Ann Nilsen was the first teacher I met on my first day at Lake Mary High School. When I was a freshman, she was my advanced keyboard (class piano) teacher. She then encouraged me to use my abilities to accompany one of her choirs the following year. This was the beginning of a relationship that has lasted eleven years to date.

There are a couple of characteristics that distinguish Mrs. Nilsen from many other teachers. She expects excellence from her students and does not settle for mediocrity. When a teacher employs this philosophy, students discover that they can perform at the highest levels, both academically and socially. The other inspirational trait that Mrs. Nilsen possesses is sincere compassion. She truly cares about students, and her actions reflect this. I distinctly remember being in the choral library one day and discovering a suicide note from a fellow student. When I showed it to Mrs. Nilsen, she dropped everything and immediately called a guidance counselor. The student was in psychiatric care within one hour. Although I am blessed with two wonderful parents who cared for my every need, many young people are not. Mrs. Nilsen fills in the gap for students who need a parental figure in their lives.

When I witnessed the impact that one person could have on the lives of others, I decided to follow in the footsteps of Mrs. Nilsen and become a music educator. As they say, imitation is the greatest form of flattery.

Lou Holtz
Football Coach, Notre Dame, University of South Carolina

I had an English teacher named Glenda Dunlop who was the toughest person I have ever met, pound for pound. She didn't weigh a hundred pounds, but was so demanding and I really disliked her for many years. I've come to appreciate the contribution she has made toward my life.

There was Dr. Schumaker at Kent State who stood approximately 5'4" and had a deformity in his legs. The love for his subject and his students is normally unmatched.

Bob Hope
Comedian

I've always had fun joking about teachers. They always make good fodder for humor, like... When I was in the fourth grade I fell in love with the teacher...which isn't too difficult to imagine.. she was 22 and I was 24 at the time.

But truly, I have great respect for teachers for they are creating the future of our country. . . indeed, the world.

Leonard Horn
President and CEO, Miss America Pageant

The teacher who had the most positive influence in my life was my grade school music teacher, Grace Pharasin. She recognized that I had some talent when I was in fifth grade, brought me out of my shell and inspired me to have enough confidence to be in drama and musical plays both in grammar school, high school and Cornell University. I have had many teachers over the years, but no one stands out like Grace Pharasin; without her and her inspiration, I might still be the shy person that I was, afraid to take chances and with no real sense of adventure.

Marilyn Horne
Opera Singer

I remember my third grade teacher from Bradford, PA, Ms. Lorena Peterson. She was not a musician, but a real music lover. She would play records and have the kids in my class dance around the room as the music moved us. Even though I was getting formal music training at home, I was impressed even then by her sheer love of listening. I hope she created as much interest in the other students as she did in me! Of course, singing became my life. But I will always remember Ms. Peterson's class and the joy that it brought to all of us.

Mike Huckabee
Governor, Arkansas

One of my teachers was actually the Student Council advisor, and though I never had her for a class, she had a great influence on me.

She believed in me and saw something in me when others probably didn't. When I was a freshman in high school (we had a 4 year high school), I was the 9th grade Student Council representative. She made me come early to school everyday and present her with my "to do" list for the day, and to go over the previous day's list to see what had been accomplished.

She was fair, but firm... she never let me get by with "adequate," but pushed for excellence in everything. She dared me to see what ought to be done rather than what had been done or what others said was possible. She made me accountable to her and to myself.

To this day, I'm a compulsive list maker...and I'm convinced that without her interest in me and help, I wouldn't be where I am today.

Her name is Anna E. Williams, and she's now retired and living in Mississippi. She and another teacher named Alex Strawn had a great impact on me.

Gale Anne Hurd
Movie Producer

The seminal teacher in my life would have to be Paul Hergesheimer, my English composition teacher at Palm Springs High School. He challenged me to master the form and then the content of the essay. It is certainly a tribute to him that I graduated Phi Beta Kappa from Stanford University with a degree in Communications!"

James E. Jacobson
Editor, *The Birmingham News*

I did have particular teachers who encouraged me to write. The first was E. Lura Moore, who taught English at Murphy High School in Mobile, Alabama, and was one of the greatest teachers

I've ever known. She didn't just *read* the classics to us; she *performed* them, brought them to life. I had her for two years and she, more than anyone, encouraged me to believe that I could write and challenged me to do so. The other teacher, also at Murphy, was Anita Grimes. She was the sponsor of the school paper and taught a journalism course, which gave me my first real look into a newsroom.

As to advice to an aspiring journalist, I would say *write*. That sounds obvious, but the more you write, the better you write. And, of course, read—study how *others* write. And listen. Observe. Take an interest in the world around you. So many bright young people, it seems to me, have retreated into themselves in recent years or have defined their interest so narrowly that they miss the thrill and satisfaction of community involvement.

Pamela Jagger
Dallas Cowboys Cheerleader

Moving to a new school could have been a very difficult transition. However, during my first day of school in Texas, I met a teacher that made the move a little smoother.

Mrs. Bobo was my freshman English teacher. She took an immediate interest in me through my writing assignments. Rather than just reading my work from a purely instructional perspective, she read the content. She even asked questions.

For example, when I wrote about upcoming *Nutcracker* ballet performances, for which I was rehearsing, she inquired about tickets and attended.

She assigned so many writing projects and I seemed to flourish. I felt comfortable with the assignments. As the new kid, I didn't have much of a voice at school. Through my writing, however, I found a new voice.

Mrs. Bobo helped me to organize my thoughts and, ultimately, my writing through creative outlines that I'd never before utilized.

Through Mrs. Bobo, I began to see myself as a writer. She promoted my writing and selected me for the honors English class for the following year. Although thrilled with the invitation I was unable to accept because I had also been selected with scholarship to a private high school for the performing arts.

Although I left the chance to attend honors English, I took with me to, yet, another school, my new found love of writing and the skills Mrs. Bobo gave me.

John Jakes
Author

First, at Nicholas Senn High School in Chicago, there was Melita Skillen – Miss Skillen, we called her. Miss Skillen ran the drama program, which I joined enthusiastically in my junior year (fancying then that I wanted a career as an actor). I was overweight and introverted in those days, but Miss Skillen taught me to stand up, speak out, and lose my fear of communicating directly in this way. Being able to speak and convey ideas has stood me in good stead in business, in promoting my writing—all the way to giving commencement addresses to audiences of 40,000 and more.

Then I owe a lot to the faculty of the English department of DePauw University, where I majored in English composition. The department head (and teacher of the junior and senior fiction writing courses) was Dr. Raymond Pence, a tough but brilliant mentor whose strong U-shaped jaw and steady gaze earned him the nickname The Bulldog. Bulldog Pence and his colleagues who taught other writing courses not only taught me specific principles, but also, encouraged the work I was already doing, in the form of selling short stories to pulp magazines that would

79

never darken the door of the English faculty lounge! The DePauw people saw what I wanted to do at that stage in my writing life, and they helped me, when others, in a similar position, might have heaped contempt on the work (and the author).

I'm forever grateful to these good people, which no doubt is the reason I remember them so vividly.

Fob James, Jr.
Former Governor, Alabama

Both of my parents were public school teachers and I saw first hand the dedication of teachers in general. I believe you are correct when you say that every successful person had a teacher at some point in life that "influenced and/or inspired them."

There were two such teachers who may be credited with any success I have enjoyed. You see, I was a young boy who did not like to go to school. There were too many more important things for a boy to do in the outdoors, like fishing, hunting, playing ball, and any other kind of sport. However, my second and third grade teachers, Miss Lois McClendon and Miss Mattie Frank Davis, had other ideas for me. They forced upon me the gift of literacy with about 24 inches of leverage from their right hand, because I did not want to learn to read! And, when I got a spanking at school, I got two more when I got home with no questions asked!

Bruce Jenner
1976 Olympic Decathlon Winner

His name is L. D. Weldon, Physical Education and Track Coach of Graceland College in Lamoni, IA.

I learned so much from L.D., not just in the classroom, but he was also a second father to me. At a time in my life when outside influences can have such a major impact on your future, L.D. was there to help me develop as a person. Not only did he encourage me and get me started in running the decathlon; he got me started in the 'race of life.'

Jay Johnson
Admiral, USN Chief of Naval Operations

I can recall a number of teachers who greatly influenced me, but the one who stands out most in my mind is Mr. Bill Smillie. Mr. Smillie was my math teacher and basketball coach. He always emphasized to his students and players that when you apply yourself, good things will happen. He also made it clear that success takes diligence and hard work. On the basketball court, he stressed positive attitude and constant teamwork as the keys to success – attributes which Mr. Smillie exemplified. He never lost his cool, was always firm but fair, and was a great team builder.

As Chief of Naval Operations, I strive to pass on these lessons to Sailors in today's Navy. Attitude, teamwork, and hard work are vital to success in any profession. I continually remind our young men and women that if they apply themselves and work together, success is guaranteed.

Larry Jones
President and Founder of Feed the Children

One English teacher in particular—Ms. Gott - made a lasting impression on me. The entire high school talked about Ms. Gott because of the amount of homework she assigned! Her idea of a lighter load during the Christmas break was to read one or TWO extra books. I can't even tell you who the other English teacher was at our school because everyone talked so much about Ms. Gott. Because her whole life seemed to be English, the students nick-named her "Gabby Gott." Lucky thing was, Ms. Gott was there for the duration – some students were lucky enough to have her as a teacher for seven years – through Junior High and Senior High! All kidding aside, Ms. Gott prepared me richly for the future. Her work ethic and study habits have been with me through the years. She demanded so much and, in return, received so much! I can't think of another teacher that I respect more than Ms. Gott for caring about my future!

Hal Kanter
Movie and TV Producer, Screenwriter

Almost seventy years ago, a young teacher in Miami, Florida's Santa Clara Elementary School encouraged me to write a composition which she then submitted to an interscholastic contest and won for me a prize that gave me the confidence to continue writing.

I regret that I do not remember that teacher's name, but consider me one of the millions who are indebted to thousands of school teachers whose names may have escaped our memories but whose dedication remains in our hearts.

Carl Karcher
Founder, Chairman Emeritus of Carl's Jr. Restaurants

I attended the first grade at Beebe School in Carey, Ohio; my teacher's name was Mr. Livingston. He did not pass me into the second grade. Then I attended Oak Grove School in Upper Sandusky, Ohio, grades one through three; my teacher's name was Antonette Lourey and I remember her to have a great sense of humor. Next, I attended Eagle School in Upper Sandusky, grades four through six; my teacher's name was Sylvia Cross and she was a good disciplinarian. I attended Salem Township School in Salem Township, Ohio grades seven and eight; my teacher's name was Gladys Guthrie McClain. She taught two classes in one room and I remember her being a very charming teacher. Although charming, she failed me in the eighth grade at which time I quit school to work on the farm with my Dad in Ohio.

In my book, *Never Stop Dreaming*, on page 138, you will see a picture of Gladys Guthrie McClain presenting me with my 8th grade certificate of completion in 1981. Wow!

Irene Kassorla, Ph.D.
Beverly Hills Psychiatrist

My memories of school are filled with happy thoughts about teachers who encouraged and inspired me: Mr. McCann, who made me feel special when he called me, 'Irene the Village Queen,' Miss Matheny, my music teacher who passed her love of music on to me; Miss Brown, who guided me in writing, producing and starring in the Senior Extravaganza – saying, "I know you can do it." All of these dear people were my mentors, my friends, my wonderful teachers.

Frank Keating
Governor, Oklahoma

Father Royden Davis was the Jesuit Priest on my hall as a Georgetown University freshman. He was the symbol and reality of integrity and humanity and a love of education. He was also intensely spiritual and taught me how to live.

Kathleen Kennedy Townsend
Lt. Governor, Massachusetts

As you well know, quality education is the foundation of a strong and productive society. It is critically important for teachers, schools, and communities to provide the tools, resources, services and instruction our young people need to grow, mature and succeed as individuals and as members of our society. One such teacher who has made a lasting difference in my life is Sister Kathryn Manahan of Stone Ridge School of the Sacred Heart in Bethesda, Maryland.

Over the years, she has remained an important and outstanding figure in my life. She was more than a teacher to me and I believe that I emerged from her class prepared with skills and knowledge that enabled me to continue to grow, learn and develop as I moved onto the next level. As a role model and mentor, she encouraged and empowered me to always do my best and to never stop short of reaching my goals. I truly appreciated her openness, kindness, sensitivity and sincerity. Her knowledge and experience, hard work, loyalty, and strength were of great value and to this day I still count her as one of my greatest and most cherished influences.

James J. Kilpatrick
Journalist, Syndicated Columnist

I cannot remember the dear lady's name, but she taught Latin at Classen High School in Oklahoma City. She had a way of throwing an eraser at any scholar who messed up on the dative case. Or was it the ablative case? Probably both. She imbued me with a love of language and syntax that has served me well for sixty years.

Dennis Kimbro
The P.Kimbro Group

The teacher that stirs my imagination the most was Mr. Charles Antanasio. We, faculty as well as students, called him "*Mr. A.*" As my sixth grade teacher at William Cullen Bryant Elementary School in Teaneck, New Jersey, he was the prototype of an effective instructor, passionate, caring, conscientious, funny, and a true role model. No matter the subject or discipline Mr. A made the day's lesson interesting and upbeat. It was Mr. A who exposed me to America's fine authors. It was Mr. A who told me of a world without any limits. As a B-school professor I only hope I can have nearly the same impact on my students that Mr. A had on me. I will always be grateful.

C. Everett Koop, M.D.
Former U.S. Surgeon General

The teachers that have stood out in my life, whether they were in grade school or graduate school, were mentors. This means they were preceptors to me and were interested not only in my being adept at the fields that they taught but also interested in me as a person. They were interested how my career integrated with other things in life that makes an individual educated in a broad sense.

I fortunately had one of these teachers in grade school, high school, college, and medical school. Although I veered pretty close to the line in scientific studies, my appreciation of art, music, fine cheese, good food, travel, and hobbies came from my mentors who broadened my perspectives and have given me a life of accomplishment and enjoyment.

Harvey Korman
Entertainer, Comedian

I had three teachers who impacted and set the course for my life's work.

My 7th grade grammar school teacher in Chicago who encouraged me to become an actor. (Kathryn Galvin)

My High School Drama teacher who was instrumental in getting me into the Goodman School of Drama in 1950 after admissions had been closed.

And my Voice and Diction teacher at Goodman who taught and inspired me to pursue the highest principles of acting and the appreciation of Shakespeare and the classic playwrights. I kept in touch with her until her death. Her name was Mary Agnes Doyle. The High School teacher was Melita Skellen who I also corresponded with til her death.

Dave Koz
Jazz Musician

When I entered Jr. High School in the seventh grade, few kids were as "dorky" as I was. Granted, this is an awkward time for most kids, but I was particularly "un-cool." My older brother and sister cautioned me away from taking the required Music History class, and advised me to instead take the Introductory Band class, where you could actually play music instead of study it.

That is where I met Mary Allyce Brown, the band teacher at Portola Jr. High School. She introduced me to the saxophone, and quite frankly, my life has never been the same.

I immediately took to the instrument, and was inspired by Mrs. Brown's innate sense of fun in the learning and playing of music. There was never any pressure, just an atmosphere of pure joy. We were making music together... however bad or out of tune it sounded! I started at the back of the sax section, and worked my way up to 1st chair – all the while, her care, compassion, and encouragement guided me along.

Upon entering Taft High School, I was further inspired by Mr. Ken Kamp - the jazz band teacher. Picking up where Mrs. Brown left off, he was completely there for me. Having been a sax player himself, he would sit with me, listen, help and advise. He encouraged me to form a jazz combo – which I did. That combo later went on to be a part of the Monterey Jazz Festival High School competition. It was Mr. Kamp who gave me the feeling that I could do just about anything, musically and otherwise.

There are many people who come through your life who guide and help you. But few in mine were as effective a motivating force than Mrs. Brown and Mr. Kamp. They taught me the importance and joy of making music, and helped me uncover my gift. And while I wouldn't say "I'm cool" – even now, at least I can say, thanks to them I am just a little less dorky! For that, I'm eternally grateful.

Kreskin
World's Foremost Mentalist

It has been my outspoken feeling through the years that it is a rather tragic commentary on modern society that the highest professionals are those of us in show business whether it be sports or entertainment when the true inspirations of modern society are the teachers. Those who instruct and guide and prepare others for life.

In fourth and sixth grades my teacher was Ms. Helen Galloway. She saw fit through all those years to set aside some eight or ten minutes, almost weekly, for me to practice my thought reading abilities with my fellow students. Unbeknownst to me, when I left grade school she personally wrote letters to a number of teachers in the junior high and high school grades urging them to encourage my abilities though she never claimed to understand them. To this day Ms. Galloway and I have remained in contact and she is a teacher who believed in me from the very beginning.

In seventh and eighth grades a Ms. Stafford was my math and social studies teacher. She took tremendous interest in my ambitions as a mentalist in show business and would sit with me sometimes an hour after school as I reflected and envisioned what I would be doing in the future. She was a wonderful storyteller of her experiences in traveling and vacationing about the world and would hold the math and social studies classes spellbound with her hypnotic personality. Truly she was an inspiration and again shared her enthusiastic belief in my future.

As I reflect on both Ms. Galloway and Ms. Stafford I wonder how many teachers today would have the time to spend sharing the interests and encouragement with a student not only during class, but also after class.

Joseph Lake
Co-founder and Executive Vice President of the Children's Miracle Network

I graduated from East High School in Salt Lake City, Utah in June of 1960. That's right, I am an old guy!

My senior year I took a class that was being offered for the first time. It was Business Law. The teacher had been a history teacher before and was really a good teacher. His name was Fred "Lefty" Bennett.

That class changed my life. I learned things that year that I still remember today. He taught us how important the law was in business. Contracts, obligations, right of buyers and sellers and he made it exciting. He gave challenging projects that taught lessons and not just subjects.

I went on to the University of Utah and got a Business Management degree and then on to U.S.C. where I got a Business Law degree. In my adult life, I have really had the opportunity of using my education in my career.

"Lefty" Bennett taught kids and not just subjects. He made me want to learn all I could from him and his class, and then... to learn all I could!

When Mick Shannon and I started the Children's Miracle Network in 1982, we could not afford an attorney to do contracts. It was my education in Business Law that allowed us to start as humbly as we did. To this day, even with an attorney, I can read and even understand contracts and letters of agreement as it pertains to the law. Thank you **Lefty Bennett** for being there for me.

John Landis
Movie Director

The two teachers I remember most vividly are my fifth grade teacher, Miss Frank, at Bellagio Road Elementary School, here in L.A., and my eighth grade math teacher Mr. Powell, at Emerson Jr. High, also here in L.A.

Mr. Powell had been severely burned on an aircraft carrier during W.W. II, and literally had the face of a monster. Even as an eighth grader I was impressed by his courage, especially as he chose to teach Junior High School kids.

Ms. Frank I remember with great fondness, as she really was the one who gave me my passion for reading. She introduced me to many wonderful books with great enthusiasm and generosity.

Jack La Lanne
Physical Fitness Expert

Actually, two teachers positively impacted my life. Mr. Overton, my 7th grade teacher and Mr. Bragg, my teacher of health.

Mr. Ken Overton, taught my 7th grade class in church school. I remember him most for his interest in his students. Constantly in a good mood, he was a giver and would talk to us at length about our problems. Believe me I had plenty, I was a skinny kid and sick all the time. Our church school did not have an athletic program but Mr. Overton made sure that he played sports with us. He often asked about our dreams for the future and encouraged us to never give up. He always assured me that although I appeared weak and little I could make up for it by trying harder and believing in myself. He said "Anything in life is possible if you make it happen." To this day, I end all of my speeches with that phrase, along with the song, "I Believe."

By the time I reached the age of 14 1/2, I was a real troublemaker, and due to doctors orders I dropped out of school for 6 months. I was underweight, had mastoid problems, boils and pimples, and shoulder braces, not to mention my failing grades. My whole life revolved around eating sugar and man processed foods. As my health deteriorated, our neighbor, Mrs. Joy, suggested that my mother take me to see Paul Bragg, a lecturer who was speaking at the Oakland City Women's Club. When my mother and I entered the auditorium there were no seats available and as we turned around to leave, Mr. Bragg said, "Ushers bring two seats and put them up here on stage." Utterly embarrassed I almost died right there. Ironically, he was to say something that changed and saved my life. He said, "my dear friends it matters not your age or your present physical condition, if you obey nature's laws, you can be born again."

Those words burned into my heart, mind, and soul. That night at home, I prayed and committed myself to a life of health and fitness. I cut out all white sugar, white flour, and became strict vegetarian. Immediately, I began a regular exercise program at the Berkley YMCA and within one month I transformed into a completely different person. My temper vanished, my energy increased dramatically, people who knew me couldn't believe it was the same person. I went back to high school, improved my grades and became captain of the football team. In my spare time, I invented equipment and had many of the local firemen and policemen in the area working out in my backyard.

Ken Overton, my favorite schoolteacher, encouraged me to try harder, believe in myself, and that anything in life is possible. Paul Bragg, not a school teacher, but my teacher, not only inspired me to study nutrition, but to buy Gray's *Anatomy*, the book that lead me to get a chiropractic degree. Paul Bragg gave me the spark that started my career. The rest is history.

Tom Landry
Former Dallas Cowboys Head Coach

It is really easy for me to single out one of my favorite teachers. Miss Frances Dushek turned 80 years old this year. She was the sweetest teacher I ever had. She convinced me that I could be a great football player, but I needed to become a great student too. It wasn't easy for her to convince me of that fact. She won out when I became an honor student—Thank the Lord for Frances Dushek.

Evelyn Lauder
Senior Corporate Vice-President, Estee Lauder Company

For the most part, there were few teachers who inspired me; most of them frightened me. They all said everything bad we did would go on our "permanent record" which would follow us all our lives. I truly believed that.

But there was one who was a thorough and demanding, but very fair person, Mrs. Laubenheimer. She always took time to guide us in life situations; always gave us interesting challenges which were tangential to our regular curriculum and was very encouraging when she heard the right answer. To "graduate," so to speak, from her class to the next grade, the 6th, was a true test of courage. Most people dreaded to learn that they would be assigned to her for the following year. However, when the year ended, I remember wishing that she could take us through the next grade.

And then it was all over. But, where is that permanent record?

Elmore Leonard
Author

All through grade school I was taught by nuns and think of them now with a feeling of affection. I liked school, so I must have liked my teachers.

In high school I was taught by Jesuits, most of them scholastics, on their way to becoming priests, and I consider this period my education. They taught me to think and ask questions, and develop a desire to learn that will continue as long as I live. We did have a few priests as teachers, for Latin and Classic Greek, and one by the name of Father Skiffington, an English instructor, who was the first person to tell me I might have a talent for writing. At the University of Detroit, after the second war, there were two English instructors who saw promise in the papers I wrote. Mr. Petit excused me from attending class; we would meet in his office to discuss 17th Century English authors and the papers I wrote for the course. Mr. Grewe was the first to encourage me to write fiction. I was graduated in 1950, but didn't begin to write stories until the following year, when I made my first sale to a magazine.

God bless the teachers who made learning a pleasure.

Eugene Lehrmann
Former President, American Association of Retired Persons

The teacher who stands out in my memory taught in a two-room rural school in Two Creeks, Wisconsin, seventy years ago. Mr. Robert R. Guse was a tough but fair task master who expected every student to live up to his expectations of what the individual was able to accomplish.

The community was part of his classroom and as a result we learned about government from our exposure to town and county board meetings. Thanks to his efforts I was motivated to become an educator and later to become involved in influencing legislative actions at all levels of government.

Richard C. Levin
President, Yale University

A couple of years ago, I was asked to speak to a group of alumni of my *alma mater*, Lowell High School in San Francisco. To prepare for the occasion, I pulled out a box of old high school writing assignments and exams. Looking them over, I was astonished by the attention paid to teaching us how to express ourselves clearly. The quantity and quality of red ink on these papers of mine was truly impressive. Fine teachers like Anne Wallach, William Worley, and Dominic Zasso must have spend hours and hours grading our papers, urging us to use words that were more precise, to say exactly what we meant to say, and to organize our thinking into coherent, tightly constructed arguments.

I also received outstanding instruction in mathematics from Ivan Barker and in physics from Carl Koenig. For years, I tried without great success to write exams in economics that were as interesting and creative as the physics exams we had at Lowell.

Carl Lewis
Winner of 8 Olympic Gold Medals in Track and Field

I had a track coach at Willingboro Junior High School in New Jersey that I remember very well. I was a 7th grader and was on the track team. Mr. Paul Minore was the coach and he had me running the anchor leg of the shuttle hurdles. At this particular meet, the team was way ahead when I ran the last leg and lost the race. The other three runners were upset and let me know it. I told the coach I would never run hurdles again. The coach agreed, but only if I would run the 100 yards in 9.5 and long jump over 25 feet. My best effort was 10.1 and 23 feet at the time. During the summer I went to the Boys Jr. Nationals and ran 9.3 and jumped 25 feet 1 inch. I never ran hurdles again!!

Shari Lewis
Puppeteer Creator of *Lamb Chop*

My Mama, a pianist, was a public school music teacher, and a great one. She was also my piano teacher, which is not such a great arrangement. Because she played so well, I was overwhelmed, and resisted practice.

When the time arrived to pick a high school, my elementary school music teacher, Mrs. Eta Morris, was not happy. She was convinced that I belonged at the High School of Music and Art, because I was clearly very musical, but my skill was nil. So she said, "For the next year, if you'll bring a bag lunch for yourself, at lunch hour each day, I'll work with you at the piano" – and she did. Knowing that this relative stranger had such confidence in me was so stimulating that I started practicing. By early spring, I realized that Music & Art was an achievable goal, and I actually started enjoying my practice. I remember making all of the other kids in the neighborhood crazy by opening my window during my practice sessions so that the notes from my piano would waft all over the neighborhood, causing all the other mothers to say, "You see? Shari practices!"

Mrs. Morris was right – Music & Art did change my life. A school where everyone felt really good about themselves and about their musical achievement was just what I needed, and the skills that I acquired have served me all my life (I played violin with Jack Benny, and my sight-reading skills have made all of my television work and conducting of orchestras possible).

Mrs. Morris has retired to Florida, and we are often in touch. She is very well aware of the impact she has had on my life – among other things, because I don't let her forget.

Art Linkletter
Entertainer

I recall an outstanding teacher who affected my thinking and therefore my life. Dr. Hammond in high school in San Diego, who was a public speaking teacher and loved to call me before the class and then spring a surprise subject for me to talk on spontaneously.

"Why coconuts have hair" was one of those! Now, as a professional speaker, I still recall the "start" he gave me, and the challenge to "ad lib" my remarks in an organized way.

Yo-Yo Ma
Cellist

When Ma was nine he studied with Leonard Rose. Rose took on a paternal role and nourished what needed to be nourished. "I was a pipsqueak of a kid, and overwhelmingly shy. I was afraid to speak to Mr. Rose above a whisper. I'd try to hide behind the cello. He was always calm, soothing, and gentle. He tried to get me to overcome my timidity by constantly urging me to sing out on the instrument. I was amazed to hear phrases coming from a fifty-year-old man such as 'Sock it to me, baby!' or, to my dismay, 'Thrill me, thrill me like my wife did this morning.'

One fall, Ma surprised Leonard Rose by arriving for his lesson wearing a leather jacket and uttering a string of swear words, "I'm embarrassed when I think of the language I used. But Mr. Rose took it in his stride and saw me through this phase. At some level, he must have been very happy to find me opening up in that way. And, for some reason, he kept his faith in me. In the early years of our lessons, he would explain every piece in advance and demonstrate his interpretation. But as time went on he gave me leeway to experiment for myself."

"When I was fifteen, after I had given a concert in Carnegie Recital Hall, he said, 'Well done. Now I'm going to give you a piece-Beethoven's C-Major Sonata-to work on entirely by yourself. I'm not going to suggest bowings, fingerings, or anything. You must go ahead, learn it, and play it for me.'

One of the hardest things a teacher can do is to give a student permission to go his own way. I'll always be grateful to Mr. Rose for that."-

Leonard Maltin
Movie and TV Critic, Author

Two teachers had a great impact on my life. The first was my homeroom and English teacher in the 7th grade, who also taught Creative Writing, my favorite course. Her name was Teri Martini. I wasn't the only student who was crazy about her, several of us had crushes, I'm sure. But the amazing thing about Miss Martini was that we liked her in spite of the fact that her classes weren't easy. She got us to work, and work hard. We wanted to please her, and we took pride in the work we did for her. She had a greater influence on me than any teacher I ever had.

When I was in high school, an English teacher named Jackie Egan took an interest in me even though I didn't have her for any classes. She liked the film-buff magazine I was editing and publishing on my own, and told me one day that she wanted me to meet a good friend of hers who was an editor at Signet Books in New York. She had a feeling we would hit it off...and we did. I took the bus from Teaneck, New Jersey into Manhattan after school one day and met Patrick O'Connor. He recognized the magazines I'd brought along, and before the end of that meeting he offered me a job editing a book of movie reviews, even though I was just seventeen years old. I'm still editing that book today, some thirty years later.

Johnny Mann
Composer, Conductor

My life has been blessed by the fact that I was fortunate enough to have received a scholarship as a choir boy to St. Paul's School for Boys in Baltimore, Maryland in 1938, which turned out to be the embryo of my musical career.

St. Paul's School for Boys (205 boys from third grade through high school) was created for the choir boys of Old St. Paul's Episcopal Church in Baltimore.

97

The school was very high on teaching the principles of honor, discipline and ethics. As a boarder, I would be allowed to go home on weekends if I accrued less than seven demerits per week. Seven or more demerits would necessitate my staying at school over the weekend and working them off.

On Friday afternoon, on reviewing the demerit list for the week, I found that only four "D's" showed up on the list when I knew that I had received 14! My conscience led me to Mr. Lewis Clark, who was the Master in Charge at the time. I confessed to him as my explanation regarding the incorrect number of "D's" shown opposite my name on the list. Mr. Clark said, "Mann, because of your honesty in reporting this truthfully to me, you are dismissed from working off your demerits. The list said four, and that's all I see." Believe me, I learned a wonderful lesson.

It is all too often that we only remember negatives in association with teachers. But to think, at the age of 70, that I have found myself repeating this story many times over to people of all ages.

Archie Manning
Former Quarterback – New Orleans Saints, Sportscaster

One of the best teachers I ever had was Cecil Holmes, my 7th grade history teacher in Drew, Mississippi. Coach Holmes was also my baseball coach and next door neighbor. He and his wife had young kids and my parents kind of played the grandparent role during their stay in Drew. Coach Holmes taught me numerous things that have been beneficial to me not only in sports but in life. He was a good Christian, family man, a hard worker and a great competitor. I was very fortunate to be associated with him during my Junior High/High School days.

David Maraniss
Journalist, Biographer

The teacher who had the most influence on me, besides my parents, was Miss Kohler, my history teacher at Madison West High School. She had many fine attributes as a teacher: she was intensely interested in her material, and she knew how to make it absorbing and understandable to her students. But what I remember most about her was that she somehow intuitively understood my interest in history and believed in me when I did not believe in myself. That, in the end, is a teacher's legacy, I think: finding the spark that lights the fire in a student.

Garry K. Marshall
Movie and TV Producer

The most influential teacher in my life was a man named Raphael Philipson. He was my adviser on the student newspaper at DeWitt Clinton High School which I attended and graduated from in the Bronx, New York.

Mr. Philipson was a stiff, straight-laced intellectual who wore a bow tie and showed absolutely no sense of humor. I was sure that people who wore suits and ties, like my father, were people who didn't laugh and Mr. Philipson seemed to support my theory. I used to stand over his shoulder and watch as he edited my sports and humor column with the grim expression of someone proofreading obituaries.

At first, I worried that Mr. Philipson was going to ruin my life with one quick stroke of his familiar blue editing pencil. But I was wrong. Instead of putting me down for my humor he tried to make it better by fixing the grammar or proposing a better phrase or word. I once wrote "Eye droppers are careless folks" and Mr. Philipson suggested changing the word "folks" to "people" to make it less provincial. His patience and attention to detail made me realize that I shouldn't be afraid of intellectuals or stuffy men and women dressed in suits and ties. They were not the enemy, as I had suspected, and years later the Mr. Philipsons of the world would prove important to my career.

Mr. Philipson not only taught me about good writing, he also showed me how important discipline was. Today, whether I'm directing a movie, writing a screenplay or producing a television series, I try to approach a project with great discipline just the way Mr. Philipson taught me.

Al Martinez
Columnist, *Los Angeles Times*, Author

Calla Monlux was not much more than five feet tall and stocky, in a pleasant sort of way. She seemed the prototype schoolteacher of the 1940s, an old maid in a long dress and sensible shoes, stern but relenting. A tiny, knowing smile glows through my memory of her like an outline in fog, characterizing everything she did. It said she was wise and gentle and liked you just for who you were.

My association with her came in the sixth grade at Lockwood School in Oakland, California, where she taught English. I was a poor kid from a broken home, burdened with a drunken, violent stepfather who found pleasure in beating me for no other reason than that I reminded him of my mother's first husband, my father.

Halfway to hell at age ten, I ran away from home frequently, stole whatever I could get my hands on, fought endlessly, and stuttered badly, all of which made me somehow special to Miss Monlux. Teachers knew more about their students then; I'm sure she knew everything about me. The stuttering was obvious. In the first few weeks of class, she inaugurated sessions of oral recitation. I tried it once but couldn't put a thought together without stammering. Miss Monlux wanted me to try again but when I refused, she relented. She had an idea. I could write what I couldn't say and turn it in to her. I have wondered since if she sensed in me a raw talent to create.

My first efforts were lame, but she saw something I didn't and encouraged me to continue. Then one evening in the spring of 1941, as the United States prepared for a war that would soon come, I sat on a hillside and watched the lights of my neighborhood blink out during an air-raid alert. I compared it to the stars going dark and wrote with a singularity of purpose I had never before experienced. Miss Monlux read it and smiled that tiny, knowing smile.

"You have a very special gift," she said, "and it can take you to a very nice future. But it needs nurturing." She sat me down after school and told me to close my eyes. Then she read me parts of a William Wordsworth poem: "I wandered lonely as a cloud/That floats on high o'er vales and hills,/ When all at once I saw a crowd,/A host, of golden daffodils;/Beside the lake, beneath the trees,/Fluttering and dancing in the breeze."

When she asked if I could see them, I said no. "Visualize," she insisted. "The sun is warm. The breeze touches you." She read the poem for me again and again, each time describing, each time demanding, each time transforming words into imagery.

And then I saw them.

The daffodils emerged in a corner of my mind all buttery and golden, and the breeze touched my face with the warmth of a baby's kiss. My eyes still closed, I described what I saw and felt, and Miss Monlux, in a tone blending pride and knowledge, said, "You've learned the most important lesson you'll ever learn about writing. You've learned to visualize. Now put on paper what you see in your heart."

I wrote with a passion that has never left, for she had defined for me not only who I was but who I would always be, forever attempting to translate into words what I visualize in my head. In so doing, she altered the course of my life ... and eliminated a stammer that she never directly addressed. She didn't have to.

Her push, and her lessons in the days that followed, allowed me to overcome a dismal childhood and gave me new tools to pursue a life free of emotional pain and physical violence. I think often of Calla Monlux and the moment she set me traveling on a new path. I see her as though it were yesterday, the small, knowing smile still glowing across the years.

The vision is clear.

Mark McEwen
CBS Early Show Weather Forecaster

I was involved in journalism in high school. I was editor of our literary magazine both junior and senior year. I was also sports editor of the school newspaper my senior year. I loved both experiences and they were quite different. Literary magazine gave me the ticket to explore poetry and prose writing more from an inner self while the sports editorship helped teach me reporting and writing about events.

My mentor - Charles Wilkerson my tenth grade English teacher. He encouraged (at that time we thought forced) us to write in a journal every day which in time began the wheels turning journalistically. It was the start of my writing career.

My advice to students is to *read everything* you can get your hands on. You have to be up on everything; you have to be *smart.* Write as often as you can, read as many great writers as you can. The more you know of the world, the more you know where *you* are.

Diana McGehee
Sculptor, Hallmark Ornaments

The one teacher that had the most impact on my life was a college professor, Dr. Weir. I started out as a commercial art major. The classes only frustrated me and I had a hard time making the connection between school and career. I took a graphics class from Dr. Weir to explore a new way of using my artistic talent. His enthusiasm, professionalism and encouragement the next four years helped me to see a bridge between just art and having a career doing something I loved. Sometimes, it just takes encouragement from someone to help you look beyond the expected and see your goal in a brand new light.

Arthur Miller
Playwright

I learned French from a teacher in a Brooklyn high school – probably the only one who ever learned French in Brooklyn. I don't know why, but I sincerely felt she had some affection for me, and the net result was that I learned French in Brooklyn. I regret very much that I have long since forgotten her name, but she was large, stood very straight and had beautiful, long hair. Another teacher was Professor Eric Walter at the University of Michigan English Department. He was the first one to tell me that I should think about becoming a writer, and I've always felt a debt toward him.

Thomas Monaghan
Founder, Domino's Pizza, Inc.

My schooling in the orphanage had begun on a high note, thanks to the inspiration of a gentle, loving teacher, Sister Berarda. She became my surrogate mother, and I flourished under her care. Sister Berarda always encouraged me, even when my ideas and aspirations seemed far-fetched. I remember telling the class that when I grew up I wanted to be a priest, an architect and a shortstop for the Detroit Tigers. The other kids laughed and said that was impossible – I couldn't be all three. Sister Berarda quieted them down and said: *"Well, I don't think it's ever been done before, Tommy, but if you want to do it, there's no reason you can't."*

Funny enough, after Sister Berarda's encouragement (and my classmates' ridicule) I went on to attend the seminary for a short time, buy the Detroit Tigers, and help design many beautiful buildings modeled after the philosophy of Frank Lloyd Wright. That is inspiring!

Carson Sonny Mullis
Model for the character Sonny Crockett on *Miami Vice*

The teacher I remember most is Mrs. Tuner from Miami Edison High, in Miami, Florida. She gave me instruction in writing that stayed with me all my life. I have written many articles and several books and she has always been at the back of my mind.

It's like she said, you can be a bum or president, the world is open to you. You're in a land where freedom gives you the right to be anything you wish.

That has always stayed with me, I've never forgotten her.

Kathy Najimy
Actress
Sister Act, Veronica's Closet

I will never forget my Women's Studies Teacher—Ms. Hall! She was so supportive of my growing feminism but always played devil's advocate so the rest of the class would form opinions on their own. I remember raising my hand and shouting out about some sexist injustice and she would just nod and wink and encourage me to continue. She rocked!

Sandra Day O'Connor
Supreme Court Justice

Like most of us, I did have a teacher who helped shape my life and who pointed me in the direction of my profession in the law. He was Harry Rathbun, a professor at Stanford University. He taught undergraduates at Stanford and he also held seminars at his home to discuss personal ethics and goals and how each of us can make a difference in this complex world of ours. He was brilliant, he was kind-indeed, almost saintly; he was inspiring; and he was a lawyer. I decided to enter law school because he demonstrated so clearly that law can be a great instrument for the social good. There were no lawyers in my family and I surely would have chosen a different path but for Professor Rathbun.

Al Pacino
Actor

I was twelve years old and this wonderful teacher, Blanche Rostein, my drama teacher in school, handed me a Bible and asked me to read the Psalms. To read them to the assembly each week in the auditorium. So, I'd read the Psalms.

Earlier on, I had a taste of the word-the power of the word. I had that feeling and it really shocked me and overwhelmed me. I thought at that point I would like to do that.

A few years later I was in Greenwich Village in New York trying to be an actor. That wonderful teacher, Blanche Rostein, she did more than that...she went that extra step.

I remember her. I have a vision of her in my South Bronx apartment in the kitchen with my grandmother. She's just sitting there, just talking to my grandmother. I don't know what she was saying, but I think it's one of the reasons I'm here today.

Because she took that extra step as teachers are wont to do from time to time. And it's very important. They really make lives happen.

I love teachers when they do their thing.

Dave Pelzer
Motivational Speaker, Author

Since kindergarten, the staff at Abraham Lincoln and Thomas Edison Elementary Schools in Daly City, California, had seen the results of my mother's alcoholic outrage.

In the beginning, my teachers gently probed me about my paper-thin, shredded clothes, my offensive body odor, the countless bruises and burns on my arms, as well as why I hunted for food from garbage cans. One day my second-grade teacher, Ms. Moss, demanded a meeting with the school principal and pleaded with him to do something to help me. The principal reluctantly agreed to intervene. The next morning Mother and the principal had a private meeting. I never saw Ms. Moss again.

Immediately after that, things went from bad to worse. I was forced to live and sleep in the downstairs garage, ordered to perform slave-like chores, and received no food unless I met my mother's stringent time requirements for her demands. Mother had even changed my name from "David" to "It," and threatened to punish my brothers if they tried to sneak me food, use my real name or even look at me.

The only safe haven in my life was my teachers. They seemed to always go out of their way to make me feel like a *normal* child. Whenever one of them showered me with praise, I cherished every word. If one of my teachers brushed up against me as he or she bent over to check my assignments, I absorbed the scent of their perfume or cologne. During the weekends, as I sat on top of my hands in the garage and shivered from the cold, I employed my secret weapon. I closed my eyes, took a deep breath and tried to picture my teacher's face. Only when I visualized my teacher's smile did I begin to feel warm inside.

But years later, one Friday afternoon, I lost control and stormed out of my fifth-grade homeroom class. I ran to the bathroom, pounded my tiny red fists against the tiles and broke down into a waterfall of tears. I was so frustrated because for months I could no longer see my saviors in my dreams. I desperately believed their life force had somehow kept me alive. But now, with no inner strength to draw upon, I felt so hollow and alone inside. Later that afternoon, once my peers scurried from the classroom to their homes or the playgrounds at hypersonic speeds, I dared myself and locked my eyes onto my homeroom teacher, Mr. Ziegler. For a fragment of time I knew he felt the immensity of my pain. A moment later I broke our stare, bowed my head in respect and turned away, somehow hoping for a miracle.

Months later my prayers were answered. On March 5, 1973 for some unknown reason, four teachers, the school nurse and the principal collectively decided to notify the authorities. Because of my condition, I was immediately placed into protective custody. But before I left, the entire staff, one by one, knelt down and held me. I knew by the look on everyone's faces that they were scared. My mind flashed to the fate of Ms. Moss. I wanted to run away and dissolve. As a child called "It," I felt I was not worth their trouble.

As always my saviors sensed my anxiety and gave me a strong hug, as if to form an invisible shield to protect me from all harm. With each warm body I closed my eyes and tried to capture the moment for all eternity. With my eyes clamped shut, I heard one of my teachers gently whisper, "No matter the outcome, no matter what happens to us, this is something we had to do. As teachers...if we can have an effect on one child's life... this is the true meaning of our profession."

After the round of good-byes, I stood paralyzed—I had *never* in all my life felt such an outpouring of emotion for me. And with tears streaming down my cheeks, I promised the staff at Thomas Edison Elementary that I would never forget them and I would do my best to someday make them proud.

Since my rescue, not a single day has passed that I have not thought about my saviors. Almost 20 years to the day, I returned to Thomas Edison Elementary and presented my teachers with the very first copies of my first book, *A Child Called "It,"* which was dedicated to them, and was published on the 20-year anniversary of my rescue—March 5, 1993. That evening my teachers sat in the front row of a capacity-filled auditorium, as I fulfilled my lifetime dream of making my teachers feel special. I looked at them, with tears now running down their faces, and said, "As a child I learned that teachers have but one goal; to somehow make a difference in the life of a child. In my case it was four teachers, my school nurse and my principal who fought and risked their careers to save the life of a child called "It." I cannot, nor will not, ever forget their courage and their conviction. Twenty years ago I made a promise to my teachers. And tonight I renew my vow. For me it is not a matter of maintaining a pledge to those who had an effect on my life. For me, it is simply a matter of honor.

Joe Queenan
Columnist, *TV Guide*

My freshman year in high school, I had a Latin teacher named Father Rattigan who was also moderator of the debating team. He taught me how clever phrasing could be used to demolish an opponent in a debate. Though Americans are always sneering that "satire is what closes on Saturday night," satire has actually been very, very good to me, as is has to Dave Barry, Molly Ivins and P.J. O'Rourke. I owe my beautiful house, my bulging bank account, and my very fulfilling career to Father Rattigan and to three teachers at St. Joseph's University in Philadelphia: Thomas Donahue (French), John Mullin (English Literature) and Dr. Schmandt (Western Civilization) whose first name I never caught. They all encouraged me to read everything I could get my hands on and to worry about writing once I had something to say. I did not have anything worth saying until I was 26. Sorry, but that's the truth.

Eddie Rabbitt
Country Singer

The one teacher who had probably the greatest influence on my life, who wasn't really a teacher, but a boiler room engineer, was my father, who raised my brother and I. Thomas Patrick Rabbitt was born in Athenry, County Galway, Ireland in 1899, coming to this country around 1924. He was a patient, kind man, who taught me to grow up with a kind, caring respect for others.

Tony Randall
Actor

My acting teacher was Sanford Meisner. He made an actor of me, taught me everything I know and I owe my life to him. But our relationship was distant. He was a cold technician. That is all I can tell you. I know that many of his thousands of students over a teaching career of 60 years would disagree with me.

Dan Rather
Chief Anchor, *CBS Evening News*

One teacher who stands out from long ago and far away is Mrs. Spencer. I was in Mrs. Spencer's class in elementary school—I couldn't have been any more than nine or ten. But she recognized that my interest in newspapers seemed to be more than fleeting. So she gave me an opportunity to become an editor and a writer.

Mrs. Spencer and I collaborated on a one-page news sheet. It was really nothing more than a newsletter at best, but we called it the school newspaper. I remember that we worked up a story about our school's Arbor Day celebrations.

Though the enterprise didn't exactly prosper (for one thing, we didn't have a typewriter), it was fun and satisfying. Mrs. Spencer helped me to realize my dream of being a reporter in a rudimentary way, which gave me a taste for more. I learned the lesson that news mattered, and it was a real thrill to see my name at the top of a story.

That newspaper was in one sense a small step for me, but it was also a very big leap from dreaming about reporting the news to actually doing it, however humbly. Mrs. Spencer saw that I had the germ of an enthusiasm for a pursuit and she nurtured it. This is what teachers do every day, all over—and I can't think of any work that is more important.

Robert Reich
Former U.S. Secretary Of Labor, Professor, Brandeis University

I was blessed with a number of wonderful teachers in primary and secondary school. The one who stands out most in my mind was my sixth grade teacher, Mr. Bill Javane. He managed to transform the classroom into a place of almost magical excitement. He was full of stories, fascinating facts, puzzles, intellectual challenges, games, philosophy, and mix. Somehow, he managed to weave all of this into and around the subjects we were required to learn that year. I remember leaving sixth grade with great regret—wondering if I would ever again have the same intellectual excitement, the same wonderment. Other teachers, in subsequent years, were good; few were even inspiring. But none quite came up to the level of Bill Javane. He made learning the most marvelous experience I could ever imagine, and for that I am eternally grateful.

Sally Ride
Former Astronaut, First United States Woman in Space

I had a love of reading and science in high school. I credit my remarkable physiology teacher at Westlake High School for stirring my interest. It was the scientific method of her approach to the class that most impressed me. I had never seen logic personified before as this teacher did.

Richard Riley
Former U.S. Secretary of Education

One teacher who made a very strong impression on me was Miss Bess Allen, my third and fourth grade teacher at Donaldson

Elementary School in Greenville, South Carolina. We were sitting in the auditorium listening to the playing of one of the students who later became a concert pianist. At that time, I was struggling with piano lessons. Miss Allen leaned over to me and said "Dick, if you work hard and practice, you could play like that." That kind of overwhelmed me. I never had any idea that I could come anywhere close to that – but she alerted me to my potential.

Deborah Roberts
Journalist, *ABC News 20/20*

I did have a wonderful teacher in sixth grade by the name of Dorothy Hardy who required me to read poetry and encouraged me to enjoy it. She stressed proper grammar and creative speaking. I still remember her classes to this day. She was an inspiration to me early in life. I often mention her during speeches which I make.

Roy Rogers
Cowboy, Actor

I would like to tell you about one of my teachers, Guy Baumgardner in Duck Run, Ohio. Guy was both a teacher and a friend to all of his pupils. He maintained contact with nearly all of them until the time he died. I would always visit him when he returned to Ohio and Guy would return the favor when he was in California.

Al Roker
Weather Forecaster, *The Today Show on NBC*

I went to St. Catherine of Siena Elementary School in St. Albans, NY. In 1965, my fifth grade teacher was Mrs. Eleanor

Fryer. She was the first Black lay teacher in the Diocese of Brooklyn.

You will never meet a more challenging and gifted teacher than Mrs. Fryer. She is from the deep South—Atlanta, to be precise. She came to us with a thick Southern accent that you could cut with a knife.

It seemed she had eyes in the back of her head. If you were talking while Mrs. Fryer was up at the blackboard, woe be unto you. With chalk in one hand and eraser in the other, she would use her radar to gauge where the offender was and whirl on a dime, hurling either the eraser or the chalk with unerring accuracy.

These were the days before teachers could not use corporal punishment, although at times it seemed more like capital punishment. Even back then, I wore thick, black-rimmed glasses. I looked like an African-American junior version of Drew Carey. Mrs. Fryer used to call me "Four-Eyes." "What's the matter, Four-Eyes," she would drawl, "You can't see the answer to the math problem?"

Now I know this may seem cruel to you. But to us, Mrs. Fryer pushed us to make sure we were prepared for an outside world that could be harsh and cruel.

We would see her on Sundays at church with her family, and she would laugh and talk and we would wonder, "Is this the same Mrs. Fryer who torments us in school?"

As we got older, we came to realize why Mrs. Fryer was so tough on us. We knew she loved us. There wasn't anything she wouldn't do for her students. She taught me and my five brothers and sisters, and we all still talk about Mrs. Fryer. And guess what? At age 80, she still is helping mold young minds. She's mellowed some, but she works at St. Catherine's as a teacher's aide for first graders.

I would not be where I am today if it wasn't for Mrs. Eleanor Fryer.

Martin Savidge
Anchor/International Correspondent, CNN

If not for the journalism/communications class that I took back in high school, I can honestly say I would not be where I am today. It was 1975, the first year the class was offered. I signed up and it changed my life! The class was simple, even basic, but opened my eyes to the exciting career that has now become a profession of which I am proud.

I have been fortunate to have had a number of mentors, but I will always be in debt to the instructor of that communications class, Dennis Kraynac. What I found worked so well was the class was not textbook oriented but experience oriented. He often had people who worked in the business come in to talk with us. Back in the classroom using the video camera and a recorder we would put together our own newscasts each of us sharing and learning the many different roles involved. Like the real world of TV news much of the class was ad-libbed. It taught me to remain flexible and that the unexpected and change could make for good stories, instead of being things to dread.

High school is a prime time for such exposure because by the time I was heading on for college I had a major leg up on my classmates since I knew what I wanted to do. I could then select a college that specialized in journalism. It was a degree from that respected school, Ohio University, that gave me a badly needed edge over the competition. So, it all goes back to that high school j-class and Mr. Kraynac.

Capt. Walter M. Schirra
Astronaut, Captain United States Navy

My second grade teacher taught me the sense and value of knowledge. I knew her through grade school and Junior High School. Mrs. Crowley, retired and passed away about two years ago. She was the one I honored when asked who influenced me the most. Not the science teachers, etc.

H. Norman Schwarzkopf
General, United States Army, Retired

When I was a senior in high school, I had an English teacher who unknowingly had a profound impact on my life. The annual school debate was about to happen when this teacher came to me and asked that I enter the debate. I explained to him that I knew nothing about debate or public speaking. He responded by encouraging me to participate with the following words: "You can do anything you set your mind to if you are willing to spend the time to become thoroughly knowledgeable in your subject and have confidence that what you are speaking is the truth. You can speak with confidence and eloquence. By doing so, you will not only entertain your audience but you will educate them as well." As a result of his encouragement, I not only entered the debate but received the award as the most outstanding speaker. Little did he know that throughout the subsequent forty-six years his advise would stand me in good stead on literally thousands of occasions when I was involved in public speaking.

Jeanne Shaheen
Governor, New Hampshire

Although many teachers come to mind, probably my favorite is Mr. Heilman, my senior English teacher at Selingsgrove High

School. He was the person who really taught me how to write well and gave me a better sense of appreciation for literature. Because of his persistence and dedication, I had the skills I needed to be successful in college and in my professional career.

Bernard Shaw
Journalist, CNN America, Inc.

Categorically, my mentor/teacher was the late THELMA R. FORD at Dunbar High School in Chicago. She was an English teacher as well as the school's debate coach and public speaking teacher.

For some reason, during the first week of my freshman year at Dunbar, she plopped down on my desk a copy of Homer's *Iliad* and said, **"I want you to read this and get to know it very well if you want to get through my courses this year."**

Our friendship lasted thirty-six years, until her death.

Donald F. Shula
Former NFL Coach, Baltimore Colts, Miami Dolphins

The teacher I remember most and who had a great influence on my personal and professional career was Father Shell. Father was a Jesuit and taught logic at John Carroll University in Cleveland, Ohio.

So many of the principles that pertain to success were learned in that class. There have been many times I've had to revert back to plain and simple logic to make important decisions. I'll always remember Father Shell and his teaching philosophy.

Kathy Smith
Fitness Expert, Kathy Smith Lifestyles

During my junior and senior year of high school at Bellevue East, Illinois, I was fortunate enough to have Geri Johnson as my physical education teacher. Ms. Johnson was a strong disciplinarian, yet she cared deeply for her students. She always expected more, and continually motivated us to reach for new levels of excellence. In a time when female athletics were not supported or encouraged, she was constantly introducing us to new sports such as field hockey and basketball. She encouraged us to find a sport we really enjoyed, and gave us the courage to really strive to excel. She planted the seed for my healthful attitude, and showed me the importance of finding an activity you really enjoy and making it a part of an active and healthy lifestyle.

Ken Stabler
Former NFL Quarterback, Oakland Raiders and New Orleans Saints

I personally have always looked at coaches as the teachers that affected me the most. Without the guidance, motivation, and direction that I received from the various coaches I've had, I can honestly say that I would not have had the successful athletic career I had on the high school, college, and professional levels.

R. L. Stine
Author

Teachers never encouraged me with my writing. In fact, they tried to get me to stop!

When I was nine years old, I discovered an old typewriter up in our attic. I dragged it down to my room and started typing little magazines and joke books on it. The magazines were supposed to be funny, and had titles like *From Here to Insanity* and *The Buffoon*. I turned out HUNDREDS of them!

I was a shy kid and not terribly social. I'd bring my little magazines and joke books into school and pass them around the class. They won a lot of attention and approval from my classmates. They also won a lot of attention from my teachers—all of it negative.

The teachers were constantly confiscating my efforts, asking me to stop bringing them (my little magazines and joke books) to school, begging me not to disrupt class with them. Of course, this served as encouragement to write even more.

I've been writing ever since. Today I am thrilled by the approval teachers have given my scary books for kids. But I have to say in all honesty that when I was in school, it was my teachers' *dis*couragement that encouraged me the most!

Keith Thibodeaux
Director, *Ballet Magnificat*, Former child star in *I Love Lucy*

As a five year old in Hollywood, Catherine Barton was a teacher assigned to me by the L.A. board of education. She was one of many teachers assigned to child actors. Working on the *I Love Lucy* show was great, but at times I felt the loneliness of being the only kid on the set. She, at times was like an oasis in a desert of adults, pressures and tension on the set. Ms. Barton was a wonderfully patient lady who always looked after my welfare. If I wasn't needed in front of the cameras, she was a friend who took me for a coke at the commissary. When I needed a break from the monotony of a day, she would bring me out to the garden area where we often looked for chameleons.

I'll always remember the kindness and peace she exhibited. The only time she ever displayed any anger was when we shot late one day and she confronted Desi on the fact that I had worked too long according to the board of education. She was patient up to that point but it was really getting late. Several years later she was appointed Ron Howard's teacher on *The Andy Griffith Show*.

I had the semi-regular part of Johnny Paul Jason, and became good friends with Ron. He told me that Miss Barton often spoke of me and told him all about me. Sadly, I learned from Ron not too long ago that Miss Barton passed away. I'll always remember my first teacher, Miss Barton, with her kind and patient spirit.

Mel Tillis
Country Singer

My most memorable school teacher was Coach Jim Maynor. He took a bunch of little skinny boys and made a good football team out of us. We were the 1951 Pahokee Blue Devils.

Coach Maynor would invite a few of us to this home for dinner from time to time. Those were great times to talk and keep things in perspective. He always had time for us.

Yes, Jim Maynor is still loved by all his students and football players today. His wife Peggy is loved just as much.

Tara Van Derveer
Coach, Stanford Cardinal Women's Basketball
Coach, 1996 Gold Medal Olympic Women's Basketball Team

My fifth grade teacher was well liked by all her students because she gave us the greatest gift possible—she made each of us feel good about ourselves. Ms. Mahoney possessed a positive energy that was reflected in the interesting projects she created which consequently provided a highly motivating learning culture. Obviously based upon her own love of books, there was tremendous emphasis placed upon reading. At the beginning of the school year, there was a bare construction paper tree. As the year progressed, each book we read became a new leaf on the tree. I remember that I got all A's, even though Ms. Mahoney was quite demanding. In spite of the rigor in her classroom, we felt that we could trust her enough to talk about the things that were important to a fifth grader. She embued a sense of confident calmness and energy that made me look forward to each school day. To me, she demonstrated her ability to connect with the students by encouraging me to bring my baby sister, Heidi, to school for show and tell.

I also recall that I was in attendance in Mrs. Mahoney's classroom the day JFK was shot.

Lillian Vernon
Founder & Chief Executive Officer, Lillian Vernon Corporation

My family immigrated to New York City shortly before World War II after we were forced to flee the Nazi threat to the homes we loved in Germany and Holland. I remember how isolating the experience of entering school in a new country was.

I was lucky to have the support of several wonderful teachers in the New York City public school system who willingly gave up their free periods to tutor and encourage me. These teachers, who I will never forget, helped me learn to read and write English, lose my accent and assisted me with my homework. I had always received good grades as a student in Europe by working hard, but when I moved to America I realized I needed extra help. If it hadn't been for the concern and patience of my teachers, I would not have mastered the English language nor would I have been accepted into New York University.

These same wonderful teachers realized that I needed to make friends and socialize with other students my age. After asking what hobbies I enjoyed and discovering my talents, my teachers arranged for me to join clubs after school where I made friends immediately and quickly assimilated into American culture.

If it hadn't been for my teachers, I would not have adjusted as well as I did to gain the self-esteem to start my mail order business. My teachers gave me the confidence to succeed, and for that I will always be grateful to them.

Mike Wallace
Senior Correspondent, *60 Minutes*

In the eighth grade at John D. Runkle school in Brookline, Massachusetts, I had a teacher we called "Miss Mitchell." She was an English teacher...but her *real* passion was grammar. And when we got upset because she pushed the importance of proper grammar on us mercilessly, we nicknamed her "Biddie" Mitchell. I'm not sure why, but it spoke satisfyingly to our impatience with her insistence on proper grammar.

I've never forgotten her nor stopped being grateful to her because she was a nag. As a result, to this day I am a grammarian *par excellence*. I know my who's from my whom's, my lies from my lays, my I's from my me's, etc., etc., etc.

Miss Mitchell, I love you.

John Williams
Composer, Laureate Conductor, Boston Pops

Robert Van Eps was one of my piano teachers during my teenage years and he was also the first to introduce me to the wonders of orchestration.

I can credit him as being the first teacher to have helped me to develop a genuine commitment to music and the laborious but joyful process of its study.

Walter Williams
Syndicated Journalist, Economics Professor, George Mason University

I did have a teacher, Dr. Martin Rosenberg, who was ruthless in his demands of students. One day he wrote a sentence on the board and asked another student to correct the error in the sentence. The student did so and when Dr. Rosenberg was about to erase the sentence, I pointed out another error. He congratulated me, telling me that I was very alert that morning. As he turned his back to erase the sentence, I commented to another classmate, in a barely audible voice, that here I am paying taxes for the teachers to teach me and I'm teaching them. Dr. Rosenberg lost it all – telling me that "teaching me is like casting pearls before the swine." His subsequent observations were even less flattering.

Needless to say, I was humiliated and embarrassed at the thought of being held in such low esteem. It marked a turning point in my life. It was my junior year, and I went from mediocre performance to graduating second in my class as salutatorian.

Tom Wilson
Cartoonist-"Ziggy"

My favorite teacher was my fourth grade teacher Miss Maylee. In addition to many things I admired about her...she was one of the first adults to validate my art.

One day while she was teaching and I was drawing, not paying any attention, I looked up from my drawing to find her standing above me. Immediately she picked up my drawing and marched me down to the principal's office. I knew I was in BIG trouble!

After waiting in the principal's outer office, I was called in to take my medicine. There on the wall beside Miss Maylee and the principal was my picture. Both congratulated me on my fine drawing and the principal asked me if he could keep it.

That was the first time my art was ever taken seriously. I'll never forget either one of them.

Danny Wuerffel
NFL Quarterback, Washington Redskins
1996 Heisman Winner

The memories about teachers and learning that stand out in my mind always involve some creative technique used to create attention to a normally boring subject. In my twelfth grade English class, the teacher, Mrs. Charlene Couvillon, asked me to read the part of "Ophelia" in Shakespeare's, *Hamlet*. When it was time to sing like a woman, it got very interesting.

Also my senior year, as an athlete, my high school football coach, Jimmy Ray Stephens, taught me about self-discipline, integrity and hard work. He also liked to have a good time. It was his birthday and we tried to dump a cooler full of water on him. It worked, but we also dropped the whole cooler on his head and he chased us around for a good while!

Coach Stephens taught me about self-discipline, integrity and hard work. These are three values I think our society needs more of. If every individual could discipline themselves to do the right thing and work hard with integrity, many of society's problems would dissipate.

Section Three: American Teachers Salute American Teachers

Carol Harle
San Antonio, Texas

Twenty plus years ago I began as a sixth grade teacher full of high expectations and dreams of grandeur. My family shared in my delight, as now I was part of the 4th generation of educators. My grandmother called one day and invited me over to her garage to pick through items she had saved from years of teaching. I remember choosing covers from *Texas Highways* magazines, poetry "ditto" sheets, holiday craft ideas, and much more. These treasured items I added to my classroom collection.

While I was there, Grandma started sharing classroom tales, which included exciting lessons and "ornery kids" episodes. She wound up her "history" of teaching by giving me a wax apple that had been on her desk all the years she taught. She told me she kept that apple on her desk to be a daily reminder to her symbolizing the essence of teaching. She shared that she believed that kids were just like apples. They came to her in all shapes and colors. Some come bruised and dull; others come shiny and bright. But no matter what they looked like, good teachers take the time to open each and every one up just right so they discover the star that is in each and every one of them.

I remembered, too how Grandma always cut an apple in half around the middle, showing the star to the grandkids before we ate them. As she shared this wisdom, I accepted the true meaning of teaching that has never left me. I, too keep an apple on my desk as the symbol of my purpose as a teacher and my quest to find the stars in all my kids.

Terry Nelson, Teacher
Muncie, Indiana

We called her "Mama Lou."

In the late 1960's, calling ANY teacher of ANY age ANYthing except Mr., Mrs. or Miss was pretty much unthinkable at our public high school in Northwestern Indiana. After all, it wasn't until my senior year in the fall of 1969 that girls were finally allowed to wear pants to school or that boys could wear sideburns extending below the middle of their ears when the outcome of the now famous Tinker Supreme Court Case recognized public high school students as real citizens in regard to freedom of expression. My journalism teacher, Mary Lou Carlson, was cool. After taking her Journalism 1 class, I knew I had to try out for staff my junior year, and continue learning from and working with her. She was young, she was single, and she had a lot of personality. She really listened to her students, and assisted us in our growth to independent thinking and problem solving outside the box.

We published a weekly newspaper, *The Mirror*, on typewriters, manually justifying the type ourselves, and developing and printing the photographs in our makeshift darkroom, all housed in the home economics room since journalism and publications did not enjoy any educational respect equivalent to "college-bound" or "state required" course work.

Putting out a weekly newspaper in 1969 was quite a time-consuming chore. On Mondays and Tuesdays, stories would be written and the rough drafts typed. On Wednesdays, story versions were revised, edited, justified and pasted up on a layout sheet; photographs captioned and proportioned to fit the paper windows attached to the layout sheets, and headlines written out and counted according to the printer's "Headline Count Chart" to be added later. On Thursdays the paper went to press, and on

Fridays we distributed the newspaper, critiqued the latest issue, planned for next week's edition, and started the cycle again.

Needless to say, we spent a lot of time after school with Mama Lou. Being a part-time home economics teacher meant she was a great cook and baker, and the treats she served the staff probably consumed half of her take home pay. We learned that she had a boyfriend we called "Farmer Brown," and we teased her incessantly about the potential marriage and family plans. In return, she knew who we were dating too, and our dates were adopted into the journalism family and pub room.

At the end of the school year, we would all celebrate our journalism and staff successes with a dress up banquet at a nice, local restaurant. The Quill and Scroll gavel would be handed to the new president of the honor group, editors announced, and awards distributed. It was an event much anticipated by newcomers to the staffs, and students nearing graduation as well.

My journalism banquet at the end of my junior year was of high emotion and mixed feelings, as I was named co-editor in chief of the newspaper, handed the gavel as the new president of the Quill and Scroll Society, and received the news that my beloved teacher's contract was not renewed because of the stories we students had written in the school newspaper.

I remember her crying when she told us the news at our banquet. I remember her cleaning out her desk drawers and file cabinets the last day of school. And I remember vowing to never like or assist the new teacher the administration would hire who would not support the students and do the administration's bidding.

Ten years later, when I was dismissed from teaching in the fifth-year of advising high school publications, I looked up those dreadful stories that had cost my adviser her job to get a handle on just what it was that was so terrible to the working of the public high school in the eyes of principals and superintendents.

In 1969 we had written to complain on the editorial page about the students having to park in a back muddy lot without pavement, while construction was going on. We had reported about an incident when students from another local high school had driven around our school and shot out the windows with a gun. And we complained about the cafeteria food.

I compared those stories of 1969 with my students' stories of 1979. One letter to the editor complained about the administration failing to pay the reward they offered for information leading to the apprehension of the vandal who had spray painted vulgarities on the inside of our school. Another story had reviewed the last 10 years of homecoming football game opponent match-ups. And, of course, there was that editorial complaining about the cafeteria food.

Regardless of the outcome of the Tinker Case, the decade had come full circle regarding high school publications and the practice of the freedoms outlined in the First Amendment.

Then in 1988 – 10 years later, the result of the Hazelwood Supreme Court Case justified the actions of many of the nation's high school principals when the decision muddied the waters of who was in control of the content of the student newspaper. Ten more years went by, and again I was within 24 hours of being fired from a second high school in 1998 when I would not submit the newspaper to the principal for prior review, although she said there were currently no problems with the publication.

Throughout my 26 years of teaching journalism and advising publications—and feeding hungry staff members at deadlines, it's remarkable how not much has really changed regarding publications, teachers and their experiences. Throughout the years I thought fondly and often about my high school adviser, Mama Lou. But for reasons that I can't even pin down, I never answered the one letter she wrote me when she read about my publication troubles in 1979.

But I kept that letter and I have it still.

Last fall, after being named the Dow Jones National Journalism Teacher of the Year, in part because of my protection of students' voices through their high school publications, I packed to attend the JEA/NSPA national journalism convention in Boston, where I would have the opportunity to address my colleagues on a lifetime of work and the importance of maintaining the students' freedoms.

But I couldn't sleep the night before I left.

It was important that I contact my high school teacher of 34 years ago. I wanted her to know the profound impact her teachings had on me, and I wanted her to be proud of me, as proud as she was of my first date with the class valedictorian when we went to prom. I was nearly out of time before I had to leave for the airport, and in a near-panic.

So I pulled out my now crumpled note from 1979 in the early morning hours, took a chance before leaving for the airport, and dialed the directory assistance number for the town from which her one letter had been sent over 20 years ago.

A man answered the phone, and I crossed my fingers as I asked him if a woman named Mary Lou who used to teach at Merrillville High School years ago lived there. She did. I hoped I was talking to "Farmer Brown."

"Tiano!" she exclaimed after I told her who I was and how she might remember me. She had not forgotten me.

Mama Lou and I talked for a few minutes, and I had to fight back tears all of the time we spoke. She had followed my teaching career throughout the decades, and was indeed "so very proud" of me. She told me she never again taught journalism after her firing, but recently retired from a smaller, rural high school where she had taught home economics. She did indeed marry "Farmer Brown," and now had two grown sons, of whom she was very proud.

She also told me she was battling her third bout of cancer.

I am so lucky she is still alive, and have plans to visit her this summer. No one can know the impact a teacher can have on a single student or group of students from being honest, respectful, caring and a little brave until they've taken the time to examine their own loves and identified who helped mold their own convictions and practices along the way.

But I know.

It was my journalism teacher of 34 years ago.

And I will never forget her.

Marge Craig
Alexandria, Virginia

Her name is Norma Wissing and she was my Latin teacher in high school. You know, the dead language that nobody takes anymore and you have to explain to everybody why on earth you were taking Latin. That was back in the 1960s when Spanish and French were both introduced to our schools as foreign language options, but my friends and I chose to take Latin. Don't ask me why, but it was one of the best decisions I ever made.

Mrs. Wissing was Miss Stahl back then and she married at the end of my junior year-you know, after studying Cicero and before Virgil's *Aeneid*. Our third year class of 10 or 12 threw a surprise shower in class (any excuse to have a party), and we were all invited to the wedding. But I haven't explained yet why she was such a special teacher.

Mrs. Wissing, (Even after all these years of corresponding with her, I can't call her Norma. It feels disrespectful), commanded respect in everything she did. Her room was in the old part of the building that actually had a raised platform for her desk. She sat about a foot higher than her students and watched over them rather than looked down upon them. She was so organized that you knew exactly what was expected of you. There was homework every night and special projects lined her walls. There was the Ides of March funeral procession and Latin competitions. On special Fridays, we'd bring in our Scrabble boards and play Scrabble in Latin.

My friends and I used to delight in being able to "get off the subject" and talk about current topics in class. She had a wonderful sense of humor and we laughed a lot in that class. We thought we were in control, but she always got us back on track when she felt it was time. We wanted to please her because she was fair, kind, and consistent. She never raised her voice. She didn't have to. There was something very reassuring about her calm demeanor. She demanded a lot, but each of us felt special under her watchful eyes. I knew I wasn't going to be conjugating verbs as a practical application in life, but I learned that young people need a sense of structure in their lives. They need to feel that someone cares about their work and cares about them as individuals.

I've been corresponding with Mrs. Wissing every Christmas since I graduated all those years ago and I've been back to West Chicago to see her twice since I graduated. True to her nature, she still lives on the same street in the same house that she did in the 1960s. She came to my wedding after graduation and I found it difficult recently to tell her about my divorce. She still says I'm special and somehow that is as reassuring now as it was back in high school. Who could ask for more than that from a teacher?

Candice Perkins Bowen, Teacher
Kent State University, Ohio

My favorite childhood "occupations": Teaching school for neighborhood kids younger than I (I even collected old ditto sheets from teachers at the end of the year!) and printing a neighborhood newspaper on my toy printing press.

One teacher finally helped me "professionalize" the journalism part and later helped me see how to combine the two.

Betty Evans, (now Hyde), was the type of teacher who attracted us to her junior high classroom after school just to chat. My friends and I wanted to play matchmaker and introduce her to Johnny Mathis because we thought they would be perfect together! (Yes, this was the 1960s and she was Black and single.) She was also the best English teacher we ever had—into hands-on projects and teamwork and even process writing long before anyone ever used those terms. She knew how to make us want to write and want to do it well.

Then she announced the addition of a special ninth grade English class for those who wanted to learn more about journalism and how to put out a new school newspaper. Thus, the *Callahan Crier* was born, and my friends and I eagerly joined the class and the staff. We learned reporting, inverted pyramids, even typing to make the columns even. (Remember—this is 1961 and the only way to justify stories was for us to type them once, adding enough slash marks at the end of each line to take up 60 spaces, then type them again and to add as many spaces as there were slash marks.) We did camera-ready paste-up and once had a page with little specks on it that were really the editor's bangs, which I had trimmed as we sat too close to the layout page and wet rubber cement!

But we also took a lot of pride in our work. We critiqued after each publication and tried to do better the next time. Many of us were ready for high school journalism and signed up for that publication, too. Did others go on to media careers? I really don't know. But then I had to decide if I wanted the hectic schedule of a reporter along with raising a family. Luckily, my decision to get out of the newsroom wasn't too traumatic. After all, Miss Evans was also the role model of an excellent journalism teacher—and I was quite satisfied to adjust my career plans and follow that route.

We still keep in touch at Christmas, and though I didn't ever help her meet and marry Johnny Mathis, I don't think she cares. She's been happily married for years and happy to have made a difference in my life as both a journalist and a teacher.

Lizabeth Walsh, Teacher
Sparks, Nevada

Ken Kucan, who taught junior English at Clark HS in Las Vegas, Nevada, was an inspiring teacher. He would do things that were out of the ordinary (like standing on a desktop to get his point across), and while he was never inappropriate, he opened some of his personal life to us and made us feel as if we were really a part of his whole life, not just his teaching life. He told us all on the first day of class that he knew we took his class so we could have "the good lunch period," which was partly true for many of us. He didn't pull any punches, and he taught me so many interesting things that made his class more than just another class to take.

When I was doing my student teaching seminar, I called him and asked him for the materials he had used to teach the *Canterbury Tales*. He had me over to the house, introduced me to his wife, and shared with me the few pieces of paper from which the lessons were drawn. I was amazed-it seemed like so much material when I was a student-it seemed huge and deep and terribly interesting, but when reduced to the few pieces of paper, it seemed small and almost insignificant. That was when I realized that it wasn't the material that was larger than life and interesting. It was the man.

As of a few years ago, he was still teaching, but at a private school called The Meadows. I am glad he is still influencing students' lives, because he sure made an impact on mine.

Linda Evanchyk and Carol Mendenhall

Ray Gen, Teacher
El Segundo, California

Dear Mrs. Pickett,

I have been meaning to write this letter for many years and when your name came up in a discussion this Christmas – I knew I had to write. I wish to express my appreciation to you for the wonderful learning experience that I had in your classroom. Back in the early seventies, I was in your Spanish and English classes in sixth grade. It was a wonderful experience.

Your teaching changed the course of my life. Prior to the sixth grade, I had always struggled academically because English was my second language. I did not begin to learn English until I reached kindergarten, and thus I was always behind in my studies. I found school to be laborious and mostly discouraging. I had some very fine teachers, but I had never really experienced joy in learning. It was not the fault of my teachers, because I was simply not ready to learn academically. The language obstacle had loomed too large before me. However, in the sixth grade I was ready to blossom under the right teacher, and you were there when I needed someone to encourage me. I had never before experienced academic success.

I remember vividly when you had the class do book reports. I read for my report a very simple book and you looked at me with your soft eyes and said to me, "Raymond, I know you can do better than this simple book." When I looked into your eyes, I sensed someone who had faith in me. You looked disappointed when I had settled for a simple book, and your statement lifted me for it spoke of confidence in me. Academic confidence was something I had seldom felt.

Your classroom had a wall chart, which depicted a scene of outer space and each student had a rocket ship with his or her name inscribed on the ship. I wanted to make my rocket rise above the others. I started reading, and I actually enjoyed it.

134

Your teaching, confidence and encouragement enabled me to succeed. I read many books and my rocket made it to the top of your chart. I learned that I could be academically successful.

I am now forty years old, and I have a family of my own. I am now the English Department Chair at El Segundo High School in Los Angeles County. I have earned two Masters degrees and am currently working on a doctorate in educational technology at Pepperdine University. Of all the fine teachers I have had in subsequent years, I look back constantly to you. You taught me the most important lesson I have ever learned; a person can succeed if he or she rises to the challenge.

I am writing this letter as a belated thank you. I hope to pass on to my students what you had taught me. I have received recognition for my work with students, and I have earned several teaching awards. I owe what success I have attained to what I learned in your classroom.

Again, I wish to express my gratitude to you. May this letter find you in good health and happiness. You have my eternal gratitude and appreciation. You have made a tremendous difference in my life and in the lives of others.

Your student always,
Ray Gen

(Mrs. Pickett passed away before I completed my doctorate, but I shall always remember her.)

Claudia Dupre Hesse, Teacher
Ft. Walton Beach, Florida

By all rights I should never have become a teacher. In kindergarten, when I stole another student's cookies for snacktime, my teacher slapped me across the face for stealing and lying about it and sent me to walk home by myself. It was a trip I'd made exactly once before! In the consideration of the vicissitudes of my life, however, that experience was a minor blip on the screen! I attended 14 different schools that included California, Maryland, Virginia, Mississippi, Georgia, Florida and even Paris; France, that is. Many wonderful teachers come to mind as I contemplate the impact they've had on my life. Mr. Brandewie who introduced me to the world through a microscope; Miss Koontz who introduced me to the world through maps; the nuns of the boarding school in Paris who introduced me to the world in French; and high school instructors, Misters "G.I.Joe" Williams and Doyle, who introduced me to the world through the humanities. My trig teacher, Mrs. Cunningham, introduced me to the world I could not master and inadvertently helped me determine my major in English when I reached college. The teacher who had the most profound impact on me, however, was Miss Elizabeth Morris at Ft. Benning Elementary School in Georgia. To understand the gifting she had as a teacher, it is important to know the circumstances surrounding my enrollment in her class.

In the summer of 1960, my three brothers and I returned from France to live with my aunt and uncle in Ft. Benning. My family was falling apart through alcoholism and, later, divorce. In a daring and selfless move, my aunt and uncle chose to take us four to live with their four and offered the first stable home life we'd ever known. The details are no longer important, but we "Dupre" kids were living with relatives of a different last name, though my cousin and brother were in the same class! Many awkward moments were spent trying to explain our living situation to a crowd that didn't know divorce to be the commonplace event it is now. Miss Morris never talked to me about all that, she just bent to the task of readying her class for life through the usual curriculum for sixth graders. We did the regulation mathematics, diagramming of sentences, social studies, spelling, *et al.* One time I lifted my desk during a spelling test to look at my words and believed she hadn't seen me. When the class was dismissed for recess, however, she called me back and looked at me with those piercing eyes of hers and said, "It's very hard, isn't it, Claudia?" I burst into tears, repented, and vowed never to cheat on anything ever again.

I remember her Halloween story, told to us in broad daylight as we sat at our desks, spellbound, and the shriek she produced at the climax of the story that made us all jump out of our skins. Deliciously scary! Later, she must have somehow sensed my fragility, my desperate need to belong, so she asked me to teach the class some French. Exhilaratingly inspiring! Our sixth grade class also put on a production of *The Music Man* and I was given the starring role of Marian Paroo. My aunt went into a frenzy sewing costumes and helping me practice. Good grief. A tune-challenged eleven-year old singing in front of the curtain on stage in front of all those people! (Good preparation for teaching, wouldn't you say?) We also did a full research paper with footnotes in ink, on lined paper. Does anyone remember how many pages it took to get the footnotes right, at the bottom of the correct page, with enough room for all the *Ibids* and *Op. Cits*? My sixth grade year was blood, sweat, and tears—not mine, but Miss Morris'.

The most important contribution Miss Morris made to my life, though, was in the growth of my faith in God. Yes, it was a public school on a military post, but if there ever was a time when I needed God, it was then. Many more years of heartache would follow, but because of Miss Morris, I found God to be a refuge and strength, a strong tower in times of trouble. She did not proselytize; she merely shared. She read to us, constantly. Among the books she read aloud was John Bunyan's *Pilgrim's Progress*, chapter by chapter. I identified with Pilgrim's struggle through the Slough of Despondency and counted his victories as my own. We memorized Psalm 91 and recited it for each other in class. What comfort those words have been, "He will give His angels charge over thee, to guard thee in all thy ways"! But, if she hadn't lived those words day in and day out in the way she treated us, it would have just been another recitation exercise. You see, Miss Morris loved me, and I knew it. I also knew she loved all the students in her class, not just me. She forged a path through the wilderness of my life and demonstrated in speech and action the way I might pass on what she had given me.

Much has been written about a student's self-esteem. What I discovered that year and have affirmed every year since then is that what I needed was self-confidence. I couldn't very well handle a hostile world with mere sympathy in my toolbox. Miss Morris made sure we knew something about the world, and could manage seventh grade when we got to it. My confidence was greatly strengthened and I knew I could endure whatever circumstances came my way. Later, I encountered inspiring professors who reiterated the message Miss Morris communicated every day: "Students won't care what you know until they know you care." It is the benchmark by which I judge all I do in the classroom.

So, thank you, Miss Morris! Thank you for blessing me with your faith, your courage, your stamina, and your love. Thank you, also, to Terry Parker High School, Jacksonville, FL, whose teachers blessed me with a scholarship generated from their own salaries that enabled me to achieve my dream of following in your footsteps. I've now taught 30 years pre-school through adulthood and have spent the last eight years teaching high school English. Whatever I am to my students, I am indebted to those who went before me, who loved me, and who bid me to grow in knowledge, ability, and faith. Standardized testing, teaching methods, and classroom management techniques will come and go, but the love of a good teacher lasts forever.

Linda Evanchyk and Carol Mendenhall

Permissions

We would like to acknowledge the following who granted permission to reprint cited material in this book. (Note: By submitting their own stories, individuals who responded to our request for a "teacher story" to be included in this compilation, agreed to have their stories printed. Therefore, their names are not listed below.)

"Gratitude to Old Teachers" from EATING THE HONEY OF WORDS by Robert Bly. Copyright © 1999 by Robert Bly. Reprinted by permission of HarperCollins Publishers, Inc.

From A REPORTER'S LIFE by Walter Cronkite, copyright © 1996 by M and SA, Inc. Used by permission of Alfred A. Knopf, a division of Random House, Inc.

Richard Dreyfuss, excerpt from remarks he made at the American Federation of Teachers convention, 1996. Used by permission of Donna Bojarsky.

"The Wind Beneath Her Wings." Reprinted by permission of Jean Harper. © 1996 Jean Harper, Appeared in Chicken Soup for the Woman's Soul. © 1996 Jack Canfield, Mark Victor Hansen, Jennifer Read Hawthorne and Marci Shimoff. Published by Health Communications, Inc.

"Profiles: A Process Larger than Oneself," by David Blum. Copyright © 1989 by David Blum. Reprinted by permission of Georges Borchardt, Inc. Originally printed in *New Yorker*, May, 1989.

"A Vision of Daffodils," by Al Martinez. First printed in Modern Maturity, Jan./Feb., 1997. Used by permission of Al Martinez.

Al Pacino, excerpt from his speech at the 2001 Golden Globe Awards. Used by permission of Pat Kingsley, PMK Public Relations.

"A Matter of Honor," by Dave Pelzer, © 1996 by Dave Pelzer. Appeared in A Fourth Course of Chicken Soup for the Soul. © 1997 Jack Canfield, Mark Victor Hansen, Hanoch McCarty and Meladee McCarty. Published by Health Communications, Inc.

Biographies

Up Close with Linda Evanchyk

Linda Evanchyk has a Master's degree in Communications from the University of West Florida. She holds a Master Journalism Educator certification from the national Journalism Education Association. She is a member of the faculty at Choctawhatchee High School in Ft. Walton Beach, Florida, where she teaches English and journalism.

Besides serving as adviser for award-winning publications, Evanchyk is a free-lance writer. Her latest contribution is in *A Miracle Strip: Through the Lens of Arturo* and *Through the Hearts of Many*, published in August, 2002, on the history of Ft. Walton Beach, Florida, her hometown. For five years she produced a monthly newspaper for the employees of the school district where she is employed, and recently published a history of Choctawhatchee High School, celebrating its 50th anniversary.

Evanchyk has received numerous teaching awards: Teacher of the Year at two high schools, Teacher of the Year for the school district, State of Florida Journalism Teacher of the Year and a Freedom Communications Newspaper in Education Teacher of the Year. She has also been named a Special Recognition Adviser and Distinguished Adviser by the Dow Jones Newspaper Fund.

She has spoken at local, state and national conferences, and her articles on scholastic journalism have appeared in several national publications including *Quill* and *Scroll* and *Communication: Journalism Education Today*. Evanchyk was profiled in the January, 2002 issue of *Teacher Magazine* for her work with scholastic journalism.

When not teaching or working on publications Evanchyk also enjoys photography. Her favorite subjects include the beautiful area in which she lives (Florida's Emerald Coast on the Gulf of Mexico) and family members.

Up Close with Carol Mendenhall

Carol Mendenhall has a Master's degree in Supervision from The University of North Florida, and is working on a Master's degree in Cultural Anthropology at the University of Texas in San Antonio. Currently, she is the Director of Instructional Staff Development in the North East Independent School District in San Antonio.

During her thirty years in education she has been a high school English teacher (her favorite job), an adjunct professor at a Florida Junior College and at The University of the Incarnate Word in San Antonio, a yearbook sponsor, a high school assistant principal, a coordinator of a district secondary gifted/talented program.

Her lifelong work has centered on the teaching/learning process. Throughout her career she has presented on various topics at local, state, national and international conferences. She has served as the President of the Texas Staff Development Council and was named Staff Developer of the Year in 2001.

One of her newest ventures also involves a partner. Together, they have formed a nonprofit organization, The Center for Reflection and Transformation. The first work of the Center was to sponsor a *Courage to Teach* seminar series. The dream for the organization is to create a place where educators can come for renewal and reflection in order to transform the world.

The most important people in her life are her husband, Terry; and her two sons, Bryan and Craig. When not working, she can be found beading, reading, or hanging out the movies.

Carol and **Linda** met in 1979 when they both were on the faculty at Raines High School in Jacksonville, Florida. Their similar personalities, teaching styles, and philosophies have helped them maintain their friendship for more than twenty years. The retirement of their principal, Jimmie Johnson, in 1996, prompted them to write this book.

Final Thoughts...

This isn't necessarily the kind of book that is meant to be read cover-to-cover in one sitting. While we certainly hope you will read all 178 entries, we know that you might want to first turn to the stories written by individuals you admire and are a fan of. Read a few stories each day. Reread some. Pick it up often.

Laugh, Cry, Be Moved-Every story in this book, in one way or another, delivers the message of how a teacher positively influenced someone's life. Some stories are humorous, while others may bring you to tears. We hope that at least one story touches your heart and moves you.

Share-As you read a story that particularly appeals to you why not share it? It just might brighten someone's day. This book is filled with snapshots of individuals as you have never seen them.

Take Action-Hopefully, you will see your own teachers in these stories. Perhaps the stories will lead you to think about the caring and inspiring teachers you have had. We would like to encourage you to let those teachers who made a positive influence in your life know that you are grateful. It may feel awkward to do so, but it will mean so much.

Let Us Hear From You! We would love to hear your thoughts on this book and its message. Let us know which stories appealed to you and any positive results from reading them. E-mail us at levanchyk@yahoo.com. Also contact us if you have a teacher story you would like to submit for possible future publication. Make sure to give us contact information for you.

Contact Us

Like Us To Make a Presentation? The authors are currently accepting invitations to make a presentation at your convention or meeting to share these stories. Please contact us concerning availability of dates and fees. E-mail: levanchyk@yahoo.com

Printed in the United States
963200003BA